FRONTISPIECE   Henry VII in the 'inner' Star Chamber with his council.
Source: Year Books of Henry VII, Richard Tottel's edition 1555, *Anni Regis Henrici septimi.*

Public Record Office Handbooks
No. 21

The Court of Star Chamber and its records to the reign of Elizabeth I

by J A Guy

READER IN BRITISH HISTORY
University of Bristol

LONDON
HER MAJESTY'S STATIONERY OFFICE

CONTENTS

Preface		vii
Abbreviations		ix
1	Star Chamber's Structure	1
2	Star Chamber Records to 1558	19
3	Star Chamber Procedure to 1558	37
4	Analysis of Star Chamber Proceedings	51
Appendices		67
Footnotes		81
Bibliography		101
Index		107

© *Crown copyright 1985*
First published 1985

ISBN 0 11 440191 8

PREFACE

A spectre haunts the Star Chamber archive. It is the restless spirit of William Hudson, the court's most eminent practitioner and its first historian. Writing about 1620, Hudson praised 'the grave judgment of the sages of the common law of England who have been abstinent in publishing their meditations and arguments in their professions'. By contrast he despised the presumption of those 'who, for fear of burying their talent, post to the press to publish to others that which they well understand not themselves'. He had in mind, of course, those who had lately dared to dictate the affairs of 'his' court.

Of writing upon Star Chamber there is no end. The court's extant records constitute a vast bulk of material, but what survives is an unbalanced portion of what once existed. The opportunities and the pitfalls are ubiquitous. This guide is not the first word on Star Chamber nor by any means will it be the last. Its *raison d'être* is to provide the sort of guide that the compiler would have appreciated when he first crossed the threshold of the Public Record Office. Those records of Star Chamber in existence by Elizabeth I's accession are described, and the Tudor court's organization and institutional structure are elucidated. Without a basic knowledge of the machinery and conventions that generated records, the modern researcher works at a disadvantage. While, therefore, the records from 1485 to 1558 are the true focus of this guide, the historical context has been outlined to 1603. For without elementary appreciation of the radical transformation that affected Star Chamber's organization and jurisdiction in the years after 1560, the study of the earlier records becomes an antiquarian, rather than an historical exercise. Yet it is the Elizabethan transformation that affords coherence to the earlier period from 1485 to 1558 and justifies its treatment here as a separate entity. The later records of Star Chamber, which are more numerous even than those that came before, will be treated in a study by Professor Thomas G. Barnes.

This guide was begun while I was an Assistant Keeper of the Public Records. I am most grateful to Dr. R. F. Hunnisett for his enduring patience in awaiting its completion. To Professor Barnes I owe a particular debt of gratitude. Matters that could not conveniently be ventilated by correspondence were eagerly debated in Berkeley, Cambridge and Bristol. Yet the arguments and errors of this guide are mine, and I accept full responsibility.

Quotations from the Ellesmere MSS. on Star Chamber are published by permission of the Director of the Henry E. Huntington Library, San Marino,

California. I gladly acknowledge the generosity of Lady Neale, who allowed me to draw upon her London M.A. thesis. The frontispiece is reproduced from Year Books of Henry VII, ed. Richard Tottel, 1555, *Anni Regis Henrici septimi*, by permission of the Syndics of Cambridge University Library.

November 1984   J.A.G.

ABBREVIATIONS

APC	*Acts of the Privy Council of England.* New series. Edited by J. R. Dasent *et al.* 46 vols. London, 1890–1964.
B.L.	British Library
C.P.R.	*Calendar of the Patent Rolls preserved in the Public Record Office.* London, 1891–.
C.S.P.D.	*Calendar of State Papers, Domestic.* London, 1856–.
H.E.H.	Henry E. Huntington Library, San Marino, California
LP	*Letters and Papers, Foreign and Domestic, of the Reign of Henry VIII.* Edited by J. S. Brewer *et al.* 21 vols. and *Addenda.* London, 1862–1932.
MS.	Manuscript
P.R.O.	Public Record Office
STC	*A Short-Title Catalogue of Books printed in England, Scotland, and Ireland, and of English Books printed abroad, 1475–1640.* By A. W. Pollard, G. R. Redgrave *et al.* 2 vols. London, 1926.
STC²	*A Short-Title Catalogue of Books printed in England, Scotland, and Ireland, and of English Books printed abroad, 1475–1640.* Second edition. Edited by W. A. Jackson, F. S. Ferguson, and K. F. Pantzer. Vol. 2 so far published. London, 1976.

Manuscripts preserved at the P.R.O. are quoted by the call number there in use. The descriptions of the classes referred to are as follows:

ASSI 16	Clerks of Assize, Norfolk Circuit, Indictments and Subsidiary Documents
C 1	Chancery, Early Chancery Proceedings
C 54	Chancery, Close Rolls
C 66	Chancery, Patent Rolls
C 82	Chancery, Warrants for the Great Seal, Series II
C 244	Chancery, Files, Corpus Cum Causa
C 263	Chancery, Files, Legal Miscellanea
CP 40	Common Pleas, Plea Rolls
E 36	Exchequer, Treasury of the Receipt, Miscellaneous Books
E 101	Exchequer, King's Remembrancer, Various Accounts
E 159	Exchequer, King's Remembrancer, Memoranda Rolls

E 163	Exchequer, King's Remembrancer, Miscellanea
E 208	Exchequer, King's Remembrancer, Brevia Baronibus
E 315	Exchequer, Augmentation Office, Miscellaneous Books
E 401	Exchequer, Exchequer of Receipt, Enrolments and Registers of Receipts
E 405	Exchequer, Exchequer of Receipt, Rolls of Receipts and Issues
E 407	Exchequer, Exchequer of Receipt, Miscellanea
PC 2	Privy Council Office, Registers
REQ 1	Court of Requests, Miscellaneous Books
REQ 2	Court of Requests, Proceedings
REQ 3	Court of Requests, Miscellanea
SP 1	State Papers, Henry VIII, General Series
SP 46	State Papers, Supplementary
STAC 1	Star Chamber Proceedings, Henry VII
STAC 2	Star Chamber Proceedings, Henry VIII
STAC 3	Star Chamber Proceedings, Edward VI
STAC 4	Star Chamber Proceedings, Mary I
STAC 5	Star Chamber Proceedings, Elizabeth I
STAC 6	Star Chamber Proceedings, Elizabeth I, Supplementary
STAC 7	Star Chamber Proceedings, Elizabeth I, Addenda
STAC 8	Star Chamber Proceedings, James I
STAC 9	Star Chamber Proceedings, Charles I
STAC 10	Star Chamber Proceedings, Miscellanea

Figures in references to *LP* are to volumes and numbers of documents; in all other cases they are to pages. Where the original of a document calendared in *LP* has been used, the reference to the manuscript is given, followed by the reference to *LP*. In transcripts, abbreviations have been extended and modern punctuation has been adopted, with the result that capitals have occasionally been put where there is none in the original; otherwise, the spelling of the manuscript has been rendered exactly. In giving dates, the Old Style has been retained, but the year is assumed to have begun on 1 January.

CHAPTER ONE
Star Chamber's Structure

Star Chamber became a separate court of law under the Tudors.[1] Its sessions
were held in the *Camera Stellata* at the palace of Westminster. This 'chamber', built for the use of the Council in the reign of Edward III, comprised
two interconnecting rooms, the 'outer' and 'inner' Star Chamber, on an
upper floor of the royal palace facing the river near to the Exchequer. The
court was based in the 'outer' room, which was furnished with benches,
cushions and a table (or board). Unlike this 'outer' room, which was open to
public access, the 'inner' Star Chamber was private. It was reserved for the
monarch's use, for the private deliberations of the Council or for the debating
of some disputed legal point. The 'inner' room had a canopied throne and
benches as its furniture. 'Star Chamber' was so described because its azure
ceilings were decorated with stars of gold leaf. The walls were hung with
tapestries and rich cloths, many of which were worked with the Tudor arms
and rose. The floors were scattered with rushes and mats.[2]

Wolsey, whose passion was building, enlarged Star Chamber out of the
proceeds of the court's fines. The 'outer' room was extended and fitted out in
a manner commensurate with the court's functions. For example, a bar was
erected at which those accused of criminal offences could be brought to
answer. An enlarged board was also provided upon which the Cardinal required blatant offenders to kneel in submission. His enemies claimed that
Wolsey was inclined to bang his fist upon this table in fits of impatience.[3]

Further alterations were made to Star Chamber's buildings in 1570–71,
1579–80, and from 1586 to 1589.[4] The improvements were designed to gain
more space, to 'wynne more lighte and ayre', and to enrich the court-room
itself. 'A greate newe Starre in wainscote' was carved and gilded on the
ceiling, together with the letters of Elizabeth I's name. Other decorations
included:

> primynge with oyle collours, a table and creaste and for paintinge the said Table
> with sundrie ritche coulers in oyle, and guildinge with fine goulde her Maiesties
> Armes and the Suppoarters with sundrie badges and other Ornamentes with the
> frame or creaste Paintinge iij Sentences in capitall letters upon the white walls in the
> Starchamber court environed with compartimentes in iij severall places.

In 1608 nine large presses of wainscot, each six feet long, eight feet high and
three feet deep were constructed against the walls of the court-room to hold
old records of proceedings. Star Chamber was next repaired in 1635–6, when

a three-light window was constructed in the side of the court-room.

By 1563 a green carpet was customarily placed upon the table when Star Chamber was in session.[5] This served to differentiate between the court's sessions and a meeting of the Privy Council held in the same room. When the Privy Council met a red carpet covered the board.[6]

The court of Star Chamber was the King's Council sitting judicially. The judges of the court were the body of councillors. It is incorrect to say that the court was founded in 1487 by Henry VII's statute against liveries and retaining (3 Henry VII, c.1), as the Long Parliament claimed when it abolished the court in 1641. The supposed title of the statute is: 'Pro camera Stellata. An Acte geving the Court of Starchamber aucthority to punnyshe dyvers mysdemeanors'. However, this title was not entered on the Parliament roll at the same time as the act. Different inks were used for the title and text: the text is written in one ink, the words 'Pro camera Stellata' in another, and the rest of the title is in a third ink and hand. On the evidence of palaeography neither the words 'Pro camera Stellata' nor the rest of the title were written much before 1550, and were perhaps added later still.[7] For Star Chamber was not irrevocably linked to the act of 1487 until Ferdinand Pulton published his *Collection of Sundrie Statutes* in 1618.[8]

The historical origins of Star Chamber were much debated in and after *Onslow's Case* (1565).[9] The question of the court's antiquity is, however, less contentious today. Scholars agree that the jurisdiction of Star Chamber sprang from that of the medieval King's Council exercised in the *Camera Stellata* under Edward III, Richard II, Henry IV, Henry VI and Edward IV. Fifteenth-century sources elucidate particularly well the extent to which the Council chamber was recognised as a forum for litigation and arbitration, especially that which could be set into a context of local disorder and subversion, perversion of justice, or official maladministration. But there was no obvious differentiation in the medieval Council chamber between administration and justice: the two functions were integrally related. This situation was inherited by Henry VII's Council in 1485.[10] Differentiation was only achieved when the structure of the King's Council itself changed under the Tudors in response to political and executive policy. The history of the court of Star Chamber is ancillary to that of the Tudor state.

The changing structure of the King's Council under Henry VII and his son is summarized in figure 1. In Henry VII's reign, the Council attendant upon the king on progress flourished apart from that at Westminster in Star Chamber. Yet the respective memberships of the two parts were interchangeable and their functions, too, were undifferentiated. For administration and justice were intermingled in the early Tudor Council.

In particular the Council which attended the king while he travelled about the country on progress, and that which met in Star Chamber during the four law terms, were still protean forms of the same institution.[11] The Council's

2   Star Chamber's Structure

Figure 1

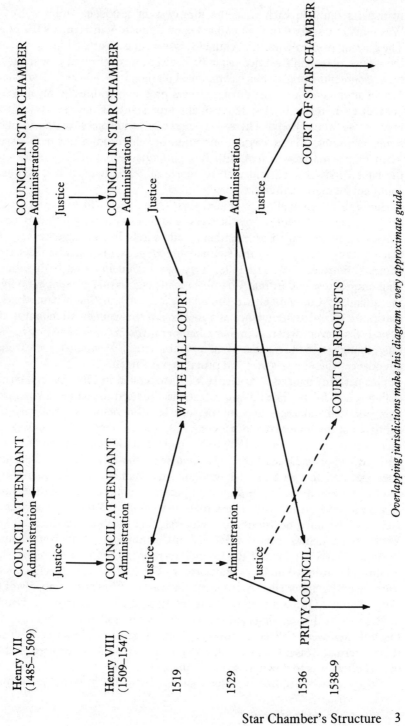

Henry VII
(1485–1509)

COUNCIL ATTENDANT
Administration

Justice

COUNCIL IN STAR CHAMBER
Administration

Justice

Henry VIII
(1509–1547)

COUNCIL ATTENDANT
Administration

Justice

COUNCIL IN STAR CHAMBER
Administration

Justice

1519

Justice

WHITE HALL COURT

Administration

1529

Administration

Justice

COURT OF STAR CHAMBER

COURT OF REQUESTS

1536

PRIVY COUNCIL

1538–9

Overlapping jurisdictions make this diagram a very approximate guide

Star Chamber's Structure   3

twin parts reunited each time the king was in residence at his palace of Westminster during term, which happened frequently in Henry VII's reign. The guiding principle was that councillors were chosen at the king's will, and the nature of a man's service depended solely on royal requirements at the time. Councillors might thus be employed on the king's affairs in Star Chamber, in attendance at Court during a royal progress, within the royal household, or even in Chancery without in any way changing their status as members of the whole body. There were not yet 'committees' of the Council, senior or junior. There was no delegation or relegation of business, except when representatives treated with foreign ambassadors. The contrast with the later Privy Council and mature courts of Star Chamber and Requests could not be more striking.

Henry VII's councillors included forty-three peers, forty-five courtiers, sixty-one clerics, twenty-seven lawyers, and forty-nine lay administrators.[12] However, more than thirty members could rarely be assembled at any one place or time, and a list of the Council attendant in 1494 mentioned sixteen names.[13] Between 1493 and 1508, forty-seven councillors sat both with the king on progress and in Star Chamber, while eight other persons sat only in the attendant Council. Other councillors sat only in Star Chamber. The maximum recorded attendance at a meeting of the Council attendant in this period was eleven, whereas in Star Chamber it rose as high as sixty-five. The king, though, was the magnet when he sat in state at Westminster: an average attendance when he was away on progress was fifteen.[14]

This pattern changed after Henry VIII's accession in 1509, though change at first came slowly. The initial context was the need to counsel a young and inexperienced monarch, and the persons best fitted for this task were the survivors of the 'inner ring' of Henry VII's Council, most of whom were also executors of his will. From 1509 to the moment of Wolsey's appointment as lord chancellor in December 1515, the discernible identities of the Council attendant and that in Star Chamber were maintained, but the institutional niceties were eclipsed by the dominant presence on both parts of the Council of some twelve members.[15] These men now comprised the close advisers of Henry VIII, taking decisions and countersigning warrants for the great seal. Yet the same men were most active in Star Chamber, too, though attendances there at plenary sessions of the Council were in no sense restricted to their group and continued much as under Henry VII.[16] However, the effect of the primacy of the 'inner ring' was to pave the way for Wolsey's monopoly of the Council after 1515, and to undermine the structure of the attendant Council of Henry VIII. For leading councillors could hardly follow the Court satisfactorily if they were obliged to commute almost daily to Westminster during the law terms. Lesser men were thus deputed to stand in as required, but the overall effect was to downgrade the Council attendant.

Wolsey's advent signalled wider changes. First, the minister reorganized the Council about himself in Star Chamber, where he presided at meetings held almost every day in term time. He reabsorbed into Star Chamber the conciliar functions exercised there and elsewhere during the previous thirty years. He maintained the size of the working Council at the levels of Henry VII's reign, but dispersed the 'inner ring' of the early years of Henry VIII. The result was to magnify Wolsey's personal power, and to give 'his' Star Chamber the capacity almost to rival Henry VIII's Court as a centre of political attention.[17] Next, Wolsey gave unprecedented emphasis to the Council's judicial function. Rarely do judges advertise their willingness to provide better justice, but Wolsey did and the impact on Star Chamber was instant. In Henry VII's reign, a mere 300 or so suits had been initiated before the Council in Star Chamber (12.5 per annum). During Wolsey's ascendancy, 1685 suits (120 per annum) were filed, a workload which was the clear consequence of ministerial encouragement.[18] For Wolsey was not shy to bring water to the mill in defiance of conventional wisdom. He was thus soon obliged to modify his scheme for the Council. Specialization both of business and personnel became the touchstone of his policy, since sophisticated management – notably differentiation and timetabling of business – had become the key to control of a system under siege from litigants. In this respect, Wolsey was the architect of the court of Star Chamber.[19]

Evidence of 580 Council meetings in Star Chamber can be discovered for Wolsey's chancellorship. In respect of 200 meetings we have some form of *acta* or minutes, and in seventy cases we have both *acta* and presence lists.[20] We find that 120 councillors served as judges in Star Chamber under Wolsey, thirty-two of whom sat at least once a week during term. The smallest reported attendance in this period was two, the highest fifty-four persons. The average daily presence varied from between eleven (frequent) to twenty-five (less usual) councillors. This format generally conforms to habits established by Henry VII's Star Chamber. Yet there was an important difference. For Wolsey began to appoint named councillors to perform the Council's judicial function, both inside and outside Star Chamber. He did so in order to free himself and the leading officers of state and household from the relentless pressure of suitors. While, then, there was no split of the component parts of the King's Council before 1529 institutionally speaking, Wolsey forged an essential distinction between the Council's executive work and justice.

Wolsey also timetabled sessions of the court of Star Chamber. In Henry VII's reign, justice and administration were freely intermingled in Star Chamber. Litigants were normally heard after the completion of the day's executive agenda. Furthermore, all aspects of legal business, however minor, were still discharged before the whole Council.[21] Faced with a vastly expanded workload in the wake of his arrival, Wolsey was persuaded of the need to organize efficiently his own and the Council's time. It was resolved in Star Chamber in June 1517 that 'the Lordes have appointed to sitt here on the

Mondaie, Tewesdaye, Thursedaye, and Satersdaie; and in the Chancery on Wensdaye and Fridaie everye weeke'.[22] This order was superseded the following October: 'For reformacion of misorders and other enormityes in the kinges severall Courtes, the Lords have appointed to assemble here everye weeke twoe dayes, that is to saye Wensdaye and Fridaie'.[23] The second order more plainly implied Wolsey's decision to differentiate between the executive and judicial work of the Council in Star Chamber. Better timetabling of the conciliar agenda was preferable to the Council's previous practices: it had become necessary to reserve two sitting days a week for hearing suits, both alleged 'enormities' and more traditional complaints. The days chosen were those adopted by the court of Star Chamber for its weekly sittings. Until abolished by the Long Parliament in 1641, Star Chamber met on Wednesdays and Fridays in term time.

Wolsey's popularization of justice was not limited to Star Chamber, however, and the impact of his advent was felt by the councillors attendant on Henry VIII, too. In 1519 Wolsey transferred most of the attendant Council's judicial function to a new sedentary court at the White Hall at Westminster. This court was given appropriate personnel, being staffed by the specialists in conciliar justice from among the former attendant councillors.[24] The court's sessions, too, were confined to the law terms, and its members only moved away to rejoin the royal progress on those very few occasions when the presence of all available councillors was required at Henry VIII's Court. Styled 'the king's most honourable Council in his Court of Requests', the White Hall Court simultaneously relieved attendant councillors of their backlog of cases at Court, while sparing suitors the inconvenience and expense of following the itinerant royal entourage.[25] Since Wolsey was soon also delegating Star Chamber business to the White Hall judges as need required, the court quickly became recognised as a separate conciliar court of justice, hearing lawsuits only, with a professional, if fluid bench, and developing its own rules of procedure. In fact, the White Hall Court under Wolsey was the immediate ancestor of the later court of Requests, which was institutionalised after two reconstructions of its personnel in 1529 and 1538.[26]

Wolsey was overthrown by an aristocratic *coup* in the summer of 1529 for failing to obtain Henry VIII's divorce. For the next ten years the Council's history merged with that of the English Reformation. Henry VIII's 'political' councillors increasingly congregated at Court where the king had reasserted overall command of his policy. The new lord chancellor was Sir Thomas More, who presided as Wolsey's successor over Star Chamber. More had little real power but he cemented Wolsey's work in the court.[27] After More's resignation, Thomas Cromwell consolidated the rejuvenated Council attendant that had re-established itself, turning it into a new executive Privy Council of reduced size. Such structural streamlining was long overdue. In fact, Cromwell merely modelled 'his' Privy Council upon an existing blueprint prepared by Wolsey in January 1526. However, the reform stuck in 1536, because the outbreak of the rebellion known as the Pilgrimage of Grace in the autumn of that year sparked a crisis that required the undivided and confidential attention of a small 'emergency' Council. This 'emergency' Council of 1536–7 and the reformed 'Privy Council' were directly related.[28]

Cromwell was himself destroyed in a Court *coup* during July 1540. Twelve days after his execution, the Privy Council met and declared its hand:

> That there shuld be a clerk attendaunt upon the sayde Counsaill to writte, entre and registre all such decrees, determinacions, lettres and other such thinges as he shuld be appoynted to entre in a booke to remayne alwayes as a leger aswell for the discardge of the sayde Counsaillors touching such thinges as they shuld passe from tyme to tyme, as alsoo for a memoriall unto them of their owne procedinges, unto the whiche office William Paget, late the Quenes Secretary, was appointed by the kinges highnes, and sworne in the presence of the sayde Counsaill the daye and yere abovesayde.[29]

In other words, the Privy Council had come of age. Specialising in administration, it abandoned the old, undivided Council's secretariat and registers in Star Chamber.[30] It began its own series of Privy Council registers and appointed a clerk. In consequence, the old Council registers became exclusively those of the court of Star Chamber, and the old Council's clerk became sole law clerk to a sole law court. Yet no division of personnel within the Privy Council itself accompanied the institutional bifurcation of the Privy Council and court of Star Chamber. In this respect the English body differed from the French *Conseil du Roi*.[31] The judges of Star Chamber in August 1540 were the nineteen privy councillors listed on the opening page of the new Privy Council register. Second-rank former members of the unreformed Council now became 'ordinary councillors' or 'councillors at large', enjoying honorific status during their lifetimes, while being employed in attendance on the monarch to sift through suits and petitions and to pass them on to the Privy Council or courts of Star Chamber or Requests for appropriate action. However, privy councillors sitting as judges in Star Chamber needed expert legal advice, as had their councillor-predecessors under Wolsey. The chief justices of King's Bench and Common Pleas thus remained full members of the bench of Star Chamber alongside privy councillors.[32]

Thereafter the standard composition of Star Chamber's bench was the Privy Council of the day together with the expert justices. This arrangement stood in force from 1540 until Star Chamber's abolition in 1641.[33] Yet it was the creation of the new Privy Council which had settled the court of Star Chamber, not the other way round. It followed that there were exceptions to the general rule restricting membership to privy councillors and chief justices. From February 1540 to May 1544, for instance, a number of former councillors or puisne justices who were not privy councillors sat as full judges in the court of Star Chamber.[34] This tendency was still evident in Elizabeth's reign, when a handful of persons who were neither privy councillors nor justices sat in 1558, 1559, 1564, 1565, 1574, 1581 and 1583.[35] The constitutional issue was tested in 1563 in the earl of Hertford's case, when nonconciliar barons who claimed a right to sit in the court had to be ousted by Nicholas Bacon, lord keeper of the great seal.[36] Yet Sir Thomas Smith, author of *De Republica Anglorum*, was unsure of the rules: he thought that Star Chamber's bench comprised 'the Lorde Chauncellor, and the Lordes and other of the privie Counsell, so many as will, and other Lordes and Barons which be not of the privie Counsell' plus the chief justices.[37] Insiders thought they knew better. William Mill, the Elizabethan clerk of Star Chamber, was 'often told' by his father, an attorney in the Henrician court, that 'noe man should sitt in ye Courte but if hee were sworne of the Councell, and that the Clerke of the Councell should goe unto him and declare unto him that hee ought not to sitt there but if hee were sworne'.[38] Even so this definition remains ambiguous when applied to Henry VIII's last years. Councillors 'at large', excluded from the Privy Council but sworn councillors none the less, were still within its terms, and the probability is that membership of Star Chamber was settled in the last resort not by constitutional principle (always presumed), but by practical politics. What counted was the Crown's ability to advise those it preferred not to attend Parliament, Privy Council or Star Chamber that they should stay away.

The membership of the Privy Council fluctuated between 1540 and 1558. Nineteen members were listed in August 1540.[39] Edward VI's Council as appointed by Henry VIII's last will and testament numbered fifteen persons. However, hyperactive political intrigue in the context of a royal minority and the alteration by the duke of Somerset of Henry VIII's will had enlarged the body's size to twenty-two persons by the beginning of 1548. After the overthrow of Somerset's Protectorate by the earl of Warwick in the autumn of 1549, the Privy Council was successively purged and reconstituted. By March 1552 it numbered thirty-one persons over whom Warwick (promoted duke of Northumberland) presided. During his ascendancy, Northumberland thus increased the membership of the Tudor Privy Council from rather more than twenty persons to thirty-one.[40] However, the bench of Star Chamber settled down in Edward's reign at a size of about eighteen persons, who included the chief justices of King's Bench and Common Pleas, the chief baron of the Exchequer and master of the rolls.[41]

In Mary's reign the Privy Council remained large. The total number of members between 1553 and 1558 was fifty.[42] Yet not all these served at the same time. In 1555 forty-one privy councillors were active (another two were inactive).[43] Even this picture, though, is misleading. Only nineteen of Mary's councillors attended over twenty per cent of Privy Council meetings held during their term of office. Thirteen attended over forty per cent of the

8   Star Chamber's Structure

meetings, eight over fifty per cent, and only four took part in over sixty per cent of them.[44] An average attendance at meetings in 1555 was twelve.[45] Although the registers of the court of Star Chamber are lost, rates of attendance there were evidently slightly higher. Sample presence lists extant for 1557 and 1558 establish that the bench of Star Chamber usually numbered twenty-two or so persons in those years: between sixteen and eighteen privy councillors to whom were added four or so expert judges.[46]

After Elizabeth I's accession in 1558 the size of the Privy Council reverted to that recognised in 1540. The queen's first Council numbered twenty members, and the death of Sir Thomas Cheyney and deprivation of Archbishop Heath quickly reduced this to a figure of eighteen. The Privy Council in 1586 had nineteen members; that of 1597 had dropped to eleven; that of 1601 had risen slightly to thirteen.[47] The Council's size under Elizabeth signalled the recovery of direction and strength by the Tudor monarchy after the uncertainties of the 1550s. Yet once again the structure of the bench of Star Chamber mirrored that of the Privy Council. Taking sample presence lists from seven different years between 1559 and 1583, we find that the court's bench variously numbered twenty, sixteen, fourteen, and seven members. The usual presence was between sixteen and twenty persons, and the number seldom fell below fourteen. Privy councillors and expert judges comprised between sixty-nine and one hundred per cent of those sitting. The average figure was eighty-five per cent, but this may be artificially low since two of the sampled meetings had political overtones which swelled attendances.[48] The court was accustomed to judging two or three cases at each sitting.[49]

Between 1529 and Henry VIII's death in 1547 the fully-fledged court of Star Chamber dealt with an estimated 150 suits per annum.[50] Under Protector Somerset and the duke of Northumberland business stabilised at 145 suits per annum.[51] Mary's Star Chamber tackled an average of 147 suits in each year of her reign.[52] Yet the annual total had apparently soared by the last year of Elizabeth's reign to an apex of 732 suits, an astonishing workload for the court, the eminent bench of which served effectively on a part-time basis.[53] The strain evidently proved too much, and in the reign of James I Lord Ellesmere and Bishop Williams successively attacked trivial or frivolous litigation in Star Chamber. The average number of suits for the reign fell in consequence to 358 per annum.[54]

The fortunes of Star Chamber were often linked to the attitudes of the lord chancellor or lord keeper of the day. Wolsey is the obvious example.[55] Without Sir Thomas More's work of consolidation after 1529 the court would have become swamped by suitors. More, too, played an important role in streamlining Star Chamber's procedure.[56] The next incumbent of distinction did not appear until 1558, when Elizabeth appointed Nicholas Bacon her lord keeper. Lord Chancellor Audley, who served from 1532 to 1544, was competent and hardworking but did not innovate. Yet sustained industry was perhaps preferable to new juridical developments during the period of the construction of the Privy Council.[57] By contrast Sir Thomas Wriothesley was an arrogant and irritating politician, eventually disgraced in the factional battles of Edward VI's minority. He was promoted lord chancellor in 1544 and served for three years.[58] Lord Rich followed Wriothesley's example by putting many of his judicial duties into commission between 1547 and 1551. Lord St. John and Bishop Goodrich briefly acted as caretaker lord keepers in 1547 and 1552 – both were out of their depth as judges.[59] Bishop Gardiner was Mary's first lord chancellor. However, he was too busy settling old scores and supervising the burning of heretics to perform much constructive work in Star Chamber. Archbishop Nicholas Heath came to the rescue in 1556. He paid serious attention to the court and its work, and began to unscramble the backlog of neglected business left by his immediate predecessors.[60] It is probably no accident that the bulk of the order and decree material that survives from Star Chamber for the middle of the sixteenth century dates from his period of office.

To channel correctly the flow of litigation after the separation of Star Chamber from the Privy Council in 1540, 'ordinary councillors' or 'masters of requests' were employed as need required to sort through suits and to direct them to the appropriate institution. The title 'master of requests' was not officially employed under the Tudors until January 1541, and then mainly related to the sorting of petitions or 'requests' addressed to the Crown which the 'masters' had undertaken on behalf of the Privy Council. Thus the Privy Council resolved on 6 October 1540 that household officials should no longer trouble Henry VIII at Court with petitions or suits, but should hand them in writing 'to such of his graces ordinary Counsaill as was appoynted to attende upon his Maiestyes person for those and like other purposes; which Counsaill shuld take such order in their said sutes from tyme to tyme as shall apperteyne'.[61] Many minor suits were in this way siphoned off to the court of Requests.

On the other hand, what was properly the business of the Privy Council had to be distinguished from the judicial work of the conciliar courts. The system of vetting suits reached its apogee under the early Tudors in March 1552, when four privy councillors, the two masters of requests, and one other person were expressly commissioned to sort petitions.[62] The move was but one aspect of an attempt by the duke of Northumberland to make the Privy Council's work more efficient.[63] All suits were to be submitted to the commissioners for their preliminary attention. They were to be handed in writing to one of the masters of requests, who was to remit to the king's secretaries 'enie that seme to concern the state of the Kings majestie or that is or ought to be kept private'. The remainder went to the commissioners. In essence their task was to sift through suitors' bills, and to weed out, settle quietly, or refer to arbitration in the provinces, those complaints which should not be allowed to waste the time of the Privy Council or Star Chamber. The Edwardian commissioners effectively acted as an 'overflow' court of Requests.[64]

Yet the ability of the Tudor Council to absorb the quantities of litigation which came before it in Star Chamber owed much to the dedicated service of its bureaucratic establishment. The principal officer of the court was the 'clerk of the Council', who retained this title even after the bifurcation of Wolsey's Council into the reformed Privy Council and court of Star Chamber. The clerk was appointed by letters patent at a fixed annual stipend of £26 13s. 4d.[65] He was sworn in and ceremonially admitted to his office. The order of succession of the Tudor clerks ran as follows:*[66]

John Baldeswell	30 September 1485–1492
Robert Rydon	10 May 1492–1509
John Meautis	17 October 1509–1512
Richard Eden	14 June 1512–1530
Thomas Eden	31 May 1530–1567
Thomas Marshe	14 May 1567–1587
William Mill	1 October 1587–1608

*Where known, the date of the clerk's admission to office has been preferred to that of the letters patent.

Assistant clerks of the Council in Star Chamber were normally appointed by letters patent at an annual salary of £20 until the separation of the Privy Council from Star Chamber.[67] The known succession of assistant clerks in Henry VIII's reign ran thus:[68]

Richard Eden	c. 1509–1512
Richard Lee	May 1516–c. 1530
Sir Thomas Elyot	c. 1526–May 1530 (unsalaried)

Under pressure of business, Sir Thomas Elyot, author of *The Governor*, was appointed by Wolsey to an extraordinary clerkship of the Council. He resigned the clerkship to the justices of assize for the western circuit in order to devote all his time to the work of Star Chamber.[69] On 4 May 1526 he was sworn in by Wolsey as a clerk of the Council.[70] Yet his position was an intrusion. No patent was made at the time of his appointment, and there was rivalry between Richard Eden and Elyot as to their respective seniority. Wolsey in 1528 devised a patent granting the principal clerkship to Elyot at the annual stipend of £26 13s. 4d., but this was conditional upon the surrender by Eden of his patent of 1512.[71] Eden declined to relinquish an office in which he worked with enthusiasm and from which he gained fees from litigants in addition to his salary. William Clayburgh, a master of Chancery, recognized Eden's precedence, and withheld Elyot's patent until its cancellation after Wolsey's fall.[72] In consequence, Elyot was obliged to serve in Star Chamber unsalaried, and he remained an assistant clerk, enjoying a temporary ascendancy only during Richard Eden's illness in late 1528 and early 1529.[73]

The muddle was cleared up by Sir Thomas More doubtless at Richard Eden's request. On 20 April 1530 a new patent was issued. This granted the clerkship of the Council to Richard Eden and his nephew Thomas in survivorship upon Richard's tactical surrender of his patent of 1512.[74] Richard Lee resigned his position as assistant clerk early in More's chancellorship; the *Governor*'s author was dismissed.[75] On 31 May 1530 Thomas Eden was sworn in by More and took up office as clerk.[76] Richard, having secured the succession, retired from active service.[77] Thereafter, the separation of the Privy Council from Star Chamber was presaged by the terms of Thomas Derby's appointment as assistant clerk in place of Lee. For Derby served the councillors attendant on Henry VIII at Court, not the court of Star Chamber, and by March 1538 he was styled in the accounts of the treasurer of the chamber as 'clerk of the Privy Council'.[78]

The clerk of the Council worked in Star Chamber under the direction of the lord chancellor. Richard Eden, for example, received and filed the written pleadings exhibited in the court, and prepared warrants for process and commissions. He noted entries of appearances, admissions to attorney, and affidavits made before the court. He recorded and filed the sworn statements of defendants and witnesses when taken at Westminster, and received and filed the certificates of commissioners in the country together with answers and depositions taken under their supervision. He kept minutes of proceedings, and drafted recognisances, injunctions, interlocutory orders and final decrees as required. He advised the Council during hearings of cases upon procedure, and perhaps precedent too. Finally, he copied up the *acta* for each sitting-day in the register of orders and decrees.[79]

Wolsey's chancellorship saw the increased definition of the clerk's responsibilities: by 1525 Star Chamber's workload required routine matters to be taken out of court. Three important orders of 5 February and 21 May 1527, and 12 June 1529 achieved this development. Wolsey's first two orders recognized and extended what had become existing practices: the clerk was to take sworn affidavits concerning the valid service of process in cases of non-appearance by defendants, and was to issue warrants for process of contempt. He was to take sworn affidavits concerning the indisposition of litigants and to issue warrants for the appropriate commissions of *dedimus potestatem*. He was also to admit defendants to attorney as a matter of routine except in notorious cases, or where the defendant had confessed the charge against him.[80] The third order empowered him to tax the costs of defendants dismissed from further appearance in Star Chamber in cases where the plaintiff had brought a writ of *subpoena* but then failed to file a bill of complaint.[81] The clerk and his assistants served, too, as examiners under Henry VIII, which had not happened often under Henry VII.[82]

The clerk's multifarious duties led during Elizabeth's reign to the proliferation of offices in Star Chamber.[83] Proliferation sprang from specialisation, which was first evident during Richard Eden's clerkship. In the 1520s, Eden and Lee did the drafting and copying of recognisances, injunctions, and orders and decrees. Eden took down most entries of appearance, admissions to attorney, and affidavits; the remaining few were done by Elyot, presumably during Eden's absence. Elyot was otherwise employed in recording the statements of defendants and witnesses during examinations. Competition for fees lay at the base of these arrangements. Elyot was assigned the work which, owing to the increased length of examinations, involved the greatest labour for the least remuneration in fees from parties. Yet Eden kept the minutes of Council decisions, and registered the out-of-court material prepared by himself and his assistants. He reserved to himself the writing up of the Council's decisions in the Star Chamber registers. He maintained lists of current causes, and prepared the certified copies of decrees entered in the register demanded by parties who had obtained writs of *certiorari*.[84]

The expansion of Star Chamber's business under Elizabeth I resulted in the creation of specialised 'under-clerkships'. By 1587, when William Mill assumed the principal clerkship, it was necessary to parcel out duties within the secretariat on a formal basis. Mill retained responsibility for filing bills of complaint and endorsing them with the date of receipt. He noted the date at which process was returnable, took the defendant's answer, and administered the oath. He took recognisances for appearance, listed cases in the book of hearing, and saw cases through their preliminary stages. He was also the court's oracle.[85] When a case came before the bench in open court, it might be referred to the clerk or to expert legal advisers for an opinion as to its suitability for decision. A case might be rejected, for instance, because 'there is a Certificatt of the badd disposicion of the plaintiff from fowre men of worshipp Justices of peace'.[86] In other cases, the clerk would be asked his opinion on matters of precedent, which must have kept him especially busy. In 1590 Mill was obliged to set up his own Star Chamber office in Gray's Inn.[87] Parties would accordingly resort there in the afternoons for out-of-court matters.

The 'under-clerkships' created were those of examiner, registrar and clerk of the files. Mill's appointment as clerk of Star Chamber coincided with the elevation of the inexperienced Sir Christopher Hatton to the chancellorship. It was thus relatively easy to innovate.[88] In the 1590s we find two examiners appointed in Star Chamber, 'who doe examine all defendants and witnesses and generally all persons whatsoever that are to be examined in Court either by speciall order or otherwise. And they have the Copieing of those examinations'.[89] Among those serving as examiners were Thomas Mynatt, who became deputy clerk of the court in 1609, and Thomas Harvey.[90] Next, two registrars were assigned the task of entering orders and decrees, rules upon motions, affidavits and appearances. The principal registrar entered orders and decrees, certificates upon reference, and orders for dismissal. Possibly Isaac Cotton occupied this post.[91] An 'under-registrar' entered affidavits and orders made in chambers by the clerk of the court. He also filed returned writs, and issued receipts for title-deeds or other documents produced as evidence in court.[92] The clerk of the files was responsible 'for filinge and takeinge from the file of every bill, replicacion and rejoinder . . . and for receivinge demurrers' along with other similar duties.[93]

Mill's proliferation of offices in Star Chamber inevitably caused a rumpus over fees.[94] Before 1587, the attorneys of Star Chamber had acted informally as under-clerks, copying pleadings, interrogatories and testimony in addition to representing the litigants they served in procedural matters. Thus in Henry VIII's time the attorneys might copy lengthy depositions as well as pleadings in exchange for a share of the 12d. per page that accrued to the clerk for such work.[95] Not only had Mill's new hierarchy of officials deprived the attorneys of lucrative work, it had generated additional costs for litigants who were forced to pay new fees to his examiners and registrars.[96] All this resulted in a comprehensive review of Star Chamber's internal affairs by Lord Keeper Egerton.[97] Mill, whose true offence was vanity, was brought to account by Egerton: he was obliged to write obsequious letters and even petitioned the queen.[98] A table of reduced fees was introduced in Star Chamber on 3 May 1598.[99] Yet the court's bureaucracy remained intact. The two examiners and principal registrar became sworn officers under the lord keeper's authority. They and the 'under-registrar' and clerk of the files remained until the court's abolition, being joined in James I's reign by additional 'clerks of ease'. Bureaucracy was thus the concomitant of Star Chamber's development. For each new official necessarily brought with him his own network of clerical assistants – under-clerks to the 'under-clerks'.[100]

The most important officer in Star Chamber after the principal clerk was the clerk of the process. Appointed by letters patent, the first incumbent was Sir Thomas Pope, founder of Trinity College, Oxford.[101] One imagines he was a sinecurist, since his patent authorised him to exercise the office by deputy. In any case, several under-clerks would have been required to perform the necessary duties. The clerkship was an office first created on 5 October 1532. Pope was to organize the writing, sealing and issue of writs of *subpoena*, attachments, commissions or any other legal process ordered by the Council in Star Chamber, and no-one else was henceforward to engage in such work save at the new clerk's direction.[102] Whereas Star Chamber had mainly been reliant on Chancery clerks for its legal process hitherto, a situation which had caused delays and confusion, now it had its own professional department of writs.

Pope surrendered his patent in December 1534, but a new grant was immediately issued in favour of himself and William Smyth in survivorship.[103] Pope died in January 1559, when he was succeeded as clerk by Thomas Cotton.[104] Within a year Thomas Cotton had likewise arranged to hold the clerkship jointly with his nephew Bartholomew. They were eventually succeeded by Bartholomew's son, Thomas.[105] Thus the clerkship of the process became a family business, the location of which is revealed in a Star Chamber bill of 1605.

> In all humbleness . . . sheweth and informeth Thomas Cotton of little St. Bartholomews neere west Smithfelde London, gent. That whereas for the space of these fortie yeeres last past and upwardes the office of makinge of all your majesties processes of your highnes most honourable court of Starre Chamber hathe bene and yett is kepte in the house where your majesties said subiecte nowe dwelleth, being in a place called the well yarde in little St. Bartholomews aforesaid. In which place there are and hath been some three or foure householders dwellinge in houses there that have upon a sufferance of neighbourhood sometymes used to hang a lyne crosse some part of the said yarde from one house to another to drye clothes upon. But notwithstanding the same sufferance, forasmuch as the annoyance and perill therebye was from tyme to tyme verye greate . . . one Francis Denman being an Attorney at the common Lawe coming latelie to dwell in the said well yard . . . hanged their clothes before your said subiectes gate and door, That your majesties said subiects cominge to the said office aboute theyr business in the Starre Chamber and others have been much ennoyed and indaungered by the passadge by and under the said clothes . . .[106]

Other staff of Star Chamber were the usher and attorneys. The usher held his post by letters patent without stipend. His duties were the physical maintenance of the *Camera Stellata* and to act as court crier. In return, he received 'a convenient house for his habitation' and various fees and tips. Richard Nores held the post in 1492, and Thomas Palmer was granted it in 1526.[107]

Whether or not the attorneys of Star Chamber should correctly be regarded as 'officers' of the court is debatable. Their duties were 'to looke that the cause bee duely prosecuted to the heareing without advantage and yf hee bee pressed by any Rule or order that may preiudice him in his cause to Informe counsaile to move the Courte. Hee is alsoe to write the Coppies of Billes, Answers and all pleadings and of all examinacions taken in the Country by Commission for his Client. He is alsoe to preferre the Clients cause to heareing'.[108] In other words, an attorney represented his client in routine matters of procedure: he reported to the client and liaised with counsel. Yet the attorney's duty was divided between the client and court. His fees accrued from both sources, since although he was directly retained by the former, he obtained a share of the fees charged for copying pleadings.[109] An attorney's work constantly obliged him to search the court's files, too, so that his trust and loyalty were owed in return.[110] Neither Wolsey nor Lord Keeper Egerton had qualms about asserting the court's authority over the attorneys.[111] Since attorneys were also sworn in and their number was strictly regulated by the court, it seems best to regard them as members of Star Chamber's establishment.[112]

Wolsey restricted the number of attorneys in Star Chamber to two. Under his authority it was no longer possible, as it had been in Henry VII's reign, to appoint any convenient person to be one's attorney.[113] By the general orders of 5 February and 21 May 1527, defendants were admitted to attorney after their answers and examinations as a matter of course. [114] This assured the future of the two attorneys of the 1520s, William Mill senior and John Valentine.[115] It was not the case that one attorney represented the plaintiff and the other the defendant as a matter of policy. No rule seems to have applied, and litigants might select either attorney to represent their interests. Shortly after Wolsey's fall, an attorney could expect to be retained in a minimum of twenty-one cases per term.[116]

A third attorney was appointed in or about 1592.[117] Yet by then many persons were involved in the task of representing clients, since it seems that attorneys established firms during Elizabeth's reign staffed by under-clerks. The number of attorneys' offices rose to four in or after 1608.[118] The known succession of attorneys in the sixteenth century was as follows:*[119]

William Mill senior	c. 1520
John Valentine	c. 1528
John Taverner	c. 1535
William Mill junior	c. 1555
John Goad	c. 1556
Edward Grimstone	c. 1572
William Hexte	c. 1587
Edward Wrightington	c. 1592
Walter Jones	c. 1592
Thomas Mills	c. 1592
Anthony Besson	c. 1600
John Beere	c. 1600

*This list may not be complete. The dates given are approximately those in which the attorneys began their service.

In conclusion, the messengers and steward of Star Chamber deserve mention. The messengers were the serjeant of the mace and the warden of the Fleet prison: their duties were to escort prisoners or bring in contumacious persons upon the court's request.[120] The steward was responsible for the diet of the bench. From at least Edward III's reign, substantial repasts were provided for the king's councillors at Westminster. Their avowed purpose was the 'expediting [of] the business of the king'.[121] The meals continued under the Tudors in the form of Star Chamber dinners, eaten shortly before noon on days when the court was in session. The known succession of stewards in the sixteenth century runs thus:[122]

Sebastian Hillorye	1522–1536
Richard Brown	1536–1553
William Staunton	1553–1572
John Doddington	1572–1585
Francis Guilpin	1585–1589
Nicholas Smythe	c. 1590

The steward prepared accounts for the costs of food and drink consumed, which listed the dates of dinners and the names of those persons said to have eaten them. These accounts, when extant, can thus provide valuable evidence of the membership of Star Chamber, but they are not always accurate and must be used with caution.[123]

CHAPTER TWO
Star Chamber Records to 1558

The problems which confront the users of Star Chamber records are as much archival as historical or legal. The extant records of the court constitute a great bulk of material, much of which is disordered and inaccessible. Yet what remains is a part only of what once existed. This partial state of the present archive is explicable in terms of the location of the records at the time of the court's abolition in 1641. At that time, the records were in two approximately equal halves. The proceedings to 1625 were deposited in large wainscot presses in Star Chamber itself. The order and decree books, entry books, titling books, calendars and other clerical apparatus of the seventeenth-century court, and the proceedings of the reign of Charles I were in the Star Chamber office, which was situated in the Holborn court of Gray's Inn.[1] The records which were in the office have failed to survive. What precisely happened is not known, but in 1705 a report to the House of Lords stated that the last that could be discovered of the order and decree books was that they were in a house in St. Bartholomew's Close, London.[2] The records which were stored in the Star Chamber were moved to the Chapter House at Westminster after the court's abolition. A second report to the House of Lords in 1719 noted that these documents were 'in a very great heap, undigested, without any covering from dust, or security from rats and mice'.[3] The same records now comprise the Star Chamber Proceedings, classes STAC 1–10, at the Public Record Office.

The Star Chamber Proceedings from 1485 to 1558 are contained in the classes STAC 1–4 and STAC 10 as follows:

STAC 1   Henry VII (1485–1509)
STAC 2   Henry VIII (1509–47)
STAC 3   Edward VI (1547–53)
STAC 4   Mary, Philip and Mary (1553–58)
STAC 10   Miscellanea (*c.* 1450–1641)

The documents are mainly pleadings and proofs, to which are added commissions of *dedimus potestatem*, and the certificates of the commissioners. The current means of reference are printed as two separate volumes: *List of Proceedings in the Court of Star Chamber, preserved in the Public Record Office*, vol. 1 (1485–1558), which is no. 13 in the Public Record Office Lists and Indexes series (Kraus Reprint Corporation: New York, 1963); and *Proceedings in the Court of Star Chamber, Indexes to Lists and Indexes, No. 13*, which is no. 4 in the Public Record Office Lists and Indexes Supplementary Series (Kraus

Reprint Corporation: New York, 1966). These volumes contain the class lists, with indexes to the same, in respect of STAC 1–4. With the exception of several bundles of Henrician documents in STAC 2, which remain unlisted and unavailable to the public,[4] the lists are complete for these classes. There is, however, no class list or other means of reference to the class STAC 10, except that given in appendix D below.[5]

The class STAC 1 (Henry VII) is divided into two artificial files which contain the records of 135 suits. These files are, nevertheless, incomplete: documents pertaining to more than eighty suits of the reign of Henry VII remain scattered through the Henry VIII records in STAC 2 and amongst the unsorted bundles in that class and in STAC 10.[6] The class STAC 2 (Henry VIII) comprises sixteen bound volumes and nineteen bundles of listed documents (the latter contained in sets of boxes). The total number of suits in the class is in the region of 5000. An intended nineteenth-century arrangement of the records was never completed, and the individual pleadings and proofs of particular cases are distributed through the volumes and boxes.[7] The original goal of the arrangers was to strive for a combined alphabetical filing of pleadings and proofs by the surnames of the principal plaintiffs. This task, however, proved too burdensome, and after the completion of the sixteen bound volumes, which had reached the letter G, any attempt at methodical arrangement was dropped. The class STAC 3 (Edward VI) is divided into nine bundles which contain the records of 878 suits. To these should be added 63 suits of the reign of Edward VI which have been wrongly placed amongst the Henrician records in STAC 2.[8] The class STAC 4 (Mary, and Philip and Mary) comprises eleven bundles and 757 suits, to which should be added 23 Marian cases also found in STAC 2.[9]

The extant Star Chamber records for the period 1485–1558 other than the documents in STAC 1–4 are contained in the class STAC 10.[10] STAC 10 comprises the miscellaneous material of all periods from the reigns of Henry VII to Charles I which was not included in STAC 1–9, and some material for the reign of Edward IV and the latter years of Henry VI. The class is divided into twenty-one substantial bundles, several of which are in more than one part, and is unarranged. It should be noted that the records in STAC 10 are essential to the study of the pre-1558 court of Star Chamber. The documents include the extant notes, drafts and minutes of the clerks of the Council in Star Chamber, original files of returned writs of *subpoena* for the reign of Philip and Mary, and many early pleadings and proofs (including copy-pleadings) not contained in STAC 1–4.[11] The clerks' papers range from notes concerning the issue of process, days set for appearances, admissions to attorney, recognisances, affidavits and draft injunctions, to minutes of orders and decrees. The files of writs constitute the earliest sequence of examples of the returned *subpoena* which are available to public inspection. The additional pleadings and proofs are comparable and supplementary to those which were placed in STAC 1–4; indeed, it is a mystery why they were excluded from the arrangement of those classes.

The records contained in STAC 1–4 and STAC 10 constitute the principal surviving source for the activity of the early Star Chamber. The present condition of the documents is variable. Some bundles have been well repaired in recent years, but many remain to be treated and a few boxes contain documents which are unfit for production. Some material is accessible only with the aid of ultra-violet light. But legibility is not otherwise a problem, since the pleadings were engrossed by professional scriveners for the most part, and the proofs were recorded by the clerks of the Council unless taken in the country. The pleadings consist of the plaintiff's bill of complaint or the information of the attorney-general, the defendant's answer, the plaintiff's replication, and the defendant's rejoinder.[12] Almost all pleadings were en-grossed on parchment, except those of the attorney-general which were filed on paper. The proofs comprise the statements of defendants, who underwent sworn examination, and the depositions of witnesses. Proofs, when taken in London, were recorded in paper 'books' by the clerks of the Council in Star Chamber. Defendants were increasingly examined on written interrogatories, which were submitted to the court on paper by plaintiffs. Witnesses were almost invariably examined on interrogatories. By permission of the court, the examination of defendants or witnesses, or both, might be undertaken in the country by local persons of credit acting under the authority of a commis-sion of *dedimus potestatem*. If these favours were allowed to the parties by the lord chancellor, the fruits of the commissioners' work would be returned to the court – if correctly submitted – engrossed on parchment. The records in STAC 1–4 and STAC 10 include also a quantity of other documents. Copies of proceedings in other courts, statements of title, deeds and bills of costs are to be found amongst the pleadings and proofs. The most fortuitous survival is that of certain drafts and copies of the court's orders and decrees. These are of great importance, despite their relative scarcity, since they provide evi-dence of the court's decisions. The records kept in the ill-fated Star Chamber office in Gray's Inn had included the order and decree books, which com-menced with the undifferentiated registers of the Henrician Council. After the creation of the Privy Council (in 1536) and its own registers (in 1540), the series of volumes which before had recorded the *acta* of the King's Council in its administrative and judicial capacities had continued as the order and decree books of the court of Star Chamber.[13] These missing volumes con-tained everything of importance to the student of the pre-1558 Star Chamber which is not now among the court's extant proceedings in the Public Record Office. Until the reign of Elizabeth, virtually the whole of Star Chamber's activity was recorded in the books: interlocutory orders and final decrees, orders for writs of *subpoena* or privy seal summonses, orders for commissions of *dedimus potestatem*, entries of appearances, admissions to attorney, recognisances, rules upon consent, and affidavits. As William Mill, the Elizabethan clerk of the court, observed in 1590:

> For my owne parte I have learned in this Court and therefore I have good warrant to speake it That untill of very late tyme . . . there was noething done either in the Courte publiquely or in the Inner Starr Chamber privately but it passed under the handes of my Predicessors and was entred in the bookes of entryes Remayneing of Recorde in the Court.[14]

A few papers, similar to those remaining in STAC 10 and which were formerly themselves amongst the Star Chamber records, were included in the artificial compilation of State Papers for the reign of Henry VIII at the Public Record Office. Notes of recognisances, minutes, a rough cause-list, a warrant for a writ of *dedimus potestatem*, a list of fines similar to a document found in STAC 2, and copy-pleadings are extant.[15] The papers other than the copy-pleadings are in the identified hands of the clerks of the Council in Star Chamber. There are also drafts of orders and decrees in the hands of the clerks and of counsel.[16] The State Papers, Henry VIII (SP 1) also contain material which throws light on the judicial activity of the Council and on individual suits in Star Chamber.[17] Correspondence in particular contributes considerably to the understanding of events and circumstances.[18] Other documents in the Public Record Office yield a small amount of additional information for the pre-1558 Star Chamber: the Chancery files (especially *Corpus Cum Causa* and *Legal Miscellanea*);[19] the *Brevia Baronibus* of the Exchequer, King's Remembrancer;[20] the Exchequer Receipt rolls;[21] and other documents of the Chancery and Exchequer.[22] A bound set of accounts for the dinners provided at Westminster for the King's Council in Star Chamber from 1515 to 1518 throws light on the frequency of Council meetings in these years.[23] The book is paralleled by a smaller and less complete wad of similar accounts in the State Papers, Henry VIII which run from 1524 to 1525.[24] The surviving books of the Treasurer of the Chamber (Exchequer, Treasury of Receipt, Miscellaneous Books) contain references to fines assessed in the court of Star Chamber, and indicate something of the methods of payment in the pre-1547 period.[25] Other information on the early court and its activity is scanty outside the classes STAC 1–4 and STAC 10. Only after the court's final maturity as a central criminal tribunal was Star Chamber able to make a marked impact on records other than those of its own archive.[26]

The initial problems encountered by the user of the classes STAC 1–4 and STAC 10 will be those arising from the need to date the documents and to collect together the constituent parts of individual cases. Although Star Chamber bills of complaint were correctly addressed to the sovereign, one in every ten bills was incorrectly addressed to the chancellor by name prior to 1558.[27] This can give a rough guide as to the date of inception of a suit. The survival of proofs, or a writ of *subpoena* or *dedimus potestatem*, in addition to pleadings enables a case to be dated, since depositions were headed with the precise date by the clerks of the Council, who acted as examiners, and writs were attested with the date of their issue. If proofs were taken in the country, the certificate of the commissioners would be precisely dated. The official endorsements of the successive clerks of the Council are also an important method of dating suits. Prior to 1556, one in every four bills of complaint carries an endorsement which records the issue of process and the date set for the defendant's appearance.[28] Three early clerks in Star Chamber – Robert Rydon, Thomas Elyot and Richard Lee – invariably added dates, months and regnal years to their notes, drafts and endorsements.[29] Richard Eden, the principal clerk during Wolsey's ascendancy, always noted days and months, but less usually regnal years.[30] His nephew Thomas Eden, who succeeded to a sole clerkship by virtue of his uncle's retirement in May 1530 (Thomas continued in office until 1567), followed Richard Eden's practice until 1556.[31] In that year, a requirement that the clerk should endorse the exact date of filing on the bill of complaint seems to have been introduced by Archbishop Nicholas Heath, probably in the form of a general order.[32] The endorsement on the bill had become a matter of record, and the inception of a suit commenced after Heath's order is, therefore, easily ascertained if the bill is extant. Earlier cases lacking specific information may sometimes be dated from internal evidence, or by reference to details of local or family history. Those suits which later found their way into extracts from the lost Henrician Council registers and Star Chamber order and decree books, or which were noted by Elizabethan lawyers and scholars as precedents, may be placed in accordance with the dates supplied by these sources.[33] Lastly, from the negative angle, cases may be eliminated from a particular enquiry on the basis of statements by plaintiffs in their bills concerning the exact dates of the outrages from which their particular griefs stemmed. Such dates bear no relation to the date of the commencement of the suit: bills were sometimes filed years after the events complained of. Clearly, however, such dates automatically exclude cases from belonging to earlier periods.

The need for users to identify the constituent parts of the individual suits in which they are interested arises from the failure of the Victorian arrangers of the classes STAC 1–4 to achieve this basic archival requirement. The careful scrutiny and listing of the documents in STAC 1–4 and STAC 10, and their collection into cases (at least on paper), will be the essential concomitants of any study. Success will, nevertheless, be limited. Despite the removal of the records from their wainscot presses in the Star Chamber apparently intact, it is clear that even this half of the original archive is now no longer complete.[34] The records were not properly protected in the Chapter House, and many documents had been lost or misplaced prior to the transfer to the Public Record Office. The pre-1558 records are also unbalanced: the distribution of the documents within the cases strongly favours pleadings, which were on parchment, over proofs, which were on paper. The rate of survival of the several instruments is roughly as follows:

Instrument	Approximate percentage of total pre-1558 suits in which instrument extant.
Bill	40
Answer	17
Replication	8
Rejoinder	4
Interrogatories*	6
Depositions*	8
Order or decree	2
Writ of *dedimus potestatem*	3
Certificate of commissioners	3
Others (one or more)	9

*Defendants or witnesses or both.

The damp conditions under which the records were reported to have been kept in the Chapter House are the most likely cause of the present relative scarcity of proofs. However, the prominence of bills of complaint can be accounted for only in terms of the archival work carried out by the Elizabethan officers of the court during the 1590s to ensure their proper arrangement. Evidence of this activity survives in the form of official endorsements, which are not to be confused with the clerical endorsements of the pre-1558 clerks of the Council in Star Chamber.[35] Nevertheless, these archival improvements appear not to have been extended to proceedings other than bills, at any rate as far as the pre-1558 records were concerned.[36] The prominence of bills may also reflect the extent to which suits were compromised out of court by arrangement between the parties after the filing of a complaint and the issue of a writ of *subpoena*.

It may also have been in the Chapter House that the records of other courts became muddled with those of Star Chamber. In STAC 2 and STAC 10, for example, just under 200 cases belong to the courts of Chancery, Requests or Wards and Liveries.[37] This problem of the correct identity of courts which is faced by the user of the classes STAC 1–4 and STAC 10 is, however, easier to resolve than those of dating and collecting the constituent parts of the individual suits. Most plaintiffs, addressing the king or the king and queen in Star Chamber by English bill procedure, prayed for the issue of process specifically returnable before 'your grace and the lords of your most honourable court of Star Chamber', or alternatively 'your grace and the lords of your most honourable Council in the Star Chamber'. The correct clerical endorsements on pleadings and the hands in which town depositions were recorded are conclusive evidence of curial identity.[38] The stated venue for the return of writs of *subpoena* and *dedimus potestatem* is similarly conclusive.[39] In cases where Star Chamber proofs were taken in the locality by commission, and are not therefore in a hand of one of the clerks of the Council, the returns of the commissioners have generally survived with the depositions to facilitate identification. Pleadings in Requests, unlike Star Chamber, were often on paper, and the judges there invariably endorsed their signatures on the bills of complaint.[40] Requests proofs were likewise recorded by that court's own staff, unless taken by commissioners. Chancery pleadings lack the clerical endorsements of Star Chamber.[41] Such endorsements, for this purpose, include those made in connection with the reorganisation in the 1590s. Also the vast majority of plaintiffs in Chancery, addressing the chancellor, asked for some particular remedy, such as discovery of documents, enforcement of trusts, relief from inequitable contracts, or specific performance, and based their appeal on the ground that remedy was denied them by the common law. Plaintiffs in Star Chamber, however, simply stated their grief, and requested remedy in general terms. No Chancery proofs have been wrongly included in the classes STAC 1–4 or STAC 10.

Having considered the pre-1558 Star Chamber records in the Public Record Office and their present arrangement, it is necessary to examine the several instruments themselves – the pleadings and proofs – and to indicate the various problems they individually raise. Private litigation began with a bill of complaint, which was a written petition explaining the plaintiff's grief and the wrong which he claimed the defendant had done him, and the damages he had sustained thereby. The following example was filed early in Henry VIII's reign:[42]

To the kyng our soverayn lord
Lamentably compleyneng shewith unto your highnes your true and feithfull Subiect Thomas Adene that where your seid Subiect beyng in goddes peace and your graces at Kynsulton in the countie of Cestre the second day of July last past, one Rafe Ryder, Richard Ryder, Rafe Congresse, John Ryder, John Walton and William Morgan, with other evil disposed parsons to your Subiect unknowen at Kynsulton aforseid in riotouse maner, that is to say with bowes and arrowes, billis, swordes and staves, assembled and then and there betwene ix and x[th] of the clocke in the nyght of the second day of July upon your Subiect did make a[s]sawte and hym sore bete, grevously maymed, and wounded, thrugh the whiche he was in great perill of deth, and most graciouse soverayn lord, the seid riotouse persons not with that contentid dayly do lye in wayte in dyverse and sondry places within the seid countie to murder and sle your seid Subiect, in exchueng[43] wherof he dareth not abyde in his natyve countre[44] to travell for his pore lyving, whiche is to his utter undoyng, whiche riott, unlaufull assemble and other mysdemeanor before declared, if condigne punyshement be not for the same had, shalbe a great encorigesyng[45] and perillouse example to all other evill disposed parsons hereafter disposed lykewise to offend. In tender consideracion wherof that it may please your Ma[jes]tie to graunt your severall wryttes sub pena directid to the [said] Rafe Ryder, Richard Ryder, Rafe Congresse, John Ryder, Joh[n] Walton and William

Morgan, commandyng theym by the same personally to appere before your highnes and the lordes of your honorable cowncell in the Star chamber at Westminster [at] a daye and under a payne there to answere to the premisses, and your Subiect shall daily pray to God for the prosperouse contynuaunce of your moost royall astate.

Henry Heydon[46]

Such bills, however, must be tested critically in every particular before the statements made in them are accepted. The plaintiff and his advisers natural-ly took considerable trouble to suggest that the weight of the evidence was all on his side. This means that the bill must be evaluated in conjunction with the defendant's answer, if anything resembling the truth is to be revealed. In Star Chamber, the most common ingredient in the complaint was the almost mechanical allegation of riot, forcible entry or assault, the relic of the ficti-tious *vi et armis* averments at common law, merely translated *verbatim* into the vernacular pleadings of the English bill courts with the addition of suit-able embellishments.[47] Even in the common law courts the claims that off-ences were committed *vi et armis* amounted often to legal fiction: the object was to catch the court's attention and to persuade the judges that the matter reported was within the orbit of royal jurisdiction.[48] Thus bigamy at common law was assumed to have been committed *vi et armis* whether or not there was any actual violence.[49] In Thomas Adene's case in Star Chamber, we cannot be sure from the evidence of the bill alone that 'bowes and arrowes, billis, swordes and staves' were carried by the alleged assailants; indeed we cannot even assume that the alleged assault took place. It is quite possible that such allegations merely cloaked a case of disputed title to real property, which was brought to Star Chamber by an aggrieved party under the fiction of public disorder.[50] Since the answers of the defendants in this case are not extant, it is a matter upon which we can merely speculate.

We should note, too, that many Star Chamber bills were filed throughout the Tudor period partly to gain advantage in respect of legal proceedings elsewhere, either at common law or in Chancery.[51] The purpose of a suit in Star Chamber after about 1500 might well be to advance a collateral attack by one litigant upon an opponent in furtherance of a wider strategy of litigation undertaken in several courts at once. At a given historical moment some suitors in Star Chamber were pleading to long-established areas of jurisdic-tion in the court; others probed new or developing areas with varying degrees of tentativeness; some suits were expressly filed to cross others brought by opponents in other courts for short-term advantage, and were never intended (or allowed) to progress beyond the bill of complaint; lastly, a minority of suits were earnestly pursued to judgment over many years.[52] The motivation of individual plaintiffs cannot, however, be deduced from unanswered bills of complaint, failing the discovery of parallel litigation in other courts upon the same matter or short of finding illuminating correspondence or other evidence. In this connection, the growing problem under the Tudors of a stream of frivolous suitors has to be fully recognised – plaguespots on the legal landscape who were not deterred either in Star Chamber or Chancery by the prospect of imprisonment in the Fleet, or the ultimate threat of the pillory or a flogging.[53] Frivolous suitors did not aim at the redress of the wrongs they had suffered when they came into court to file their complaints. Their object was simply to harass their opponents and to cause them as much inconvenience and expense as could possibly be contrived.

Answers to bills of complaint generally began with a statement as to the insufficiency and inaccuracy of the plaintiff's version, followed by a formal claim that, even if the plaintiff had a degree of substance in his complaint, which he had not, the proper remedy lay in a court other than Star Chamber – usually a court of common law. The defendant, saving all exceptions and advantages unto himself, would then usually proceed to declare the truth of the matter as he saw it. Answers invariably concluded with a general denial of the facts as alleged in the bill and a prayer for speedy dismissal with costs and expenses for the defendant's 'wrongful vexation'. The submission of a plea of 'not guilty' was sometimes sufficient in the reigns of Henry VII and VIII and was deemed to place the parties at issue on the matter alleged in the bill. As late as Mary I's reign a defendant in Star Chamber might file a simple plea of not guilty in answer.[54] But most defendants by the time of Wolsey's chancellorship were required to make some direct answer to the specific allegations made by the plaintiff. A mere negative in reply could be ruled insufficient by the court and an insufficient answer would have to be amended.

Answers were exhibited on oath in Star Chamber, as in the Elizabethan court of Chancery but unlike those filed before the equity side of the Exchequer.[55] The oath was:

You shall sweare That soe much of this Answer as doth Concerne your own Acts and deeds you knowe to bee true and that which doth Concerne any other mans Act you beleeve it to be true And you shall alsoe sweare to make true Answere to such Interrogatories as shall bee administered unto you concerning the Cause so helpe you God.[56]

The oath which all defendants swore to some extent ameliorates the *ex parte* nature of claims made in Star Chamber answers. Yet perjury was rampant in the English bill courts; in general the same degree of caution must be exercised in reading both bills and answers among the court's proceedings.

The second stage in the exchange of written pleadings was that of replication and rejoinder. The replication was either a short general denial of the defendant's answer, or it could be a more specific pleading in which the plaintiff traversed each point made in the answer and might introduce new facts and circumstances in support of his suit. A well-drawn replication could do much to shore up an ailing suit, although the plaintiff could not alter his basic case from that as exhibited in the bill of complaint. The defendant's rejoinder was designed to counteract the plaintiff's replication and was either a general refutation of the plaintiff's case or a more detailed and meticulous production which included new lines of approach to the disputed matter. In Elizabeth's reign, however, replications and rejoinders became relatively formal in comparison with the more flexible responses given by parties before 1558.[57] Sometimes they were omitted, and when they were filed they often comprised little more than a lengthy repetition of the arguments adduced in the bill of complaint and answer. The reason was that Star Chamber during the 1560s was finally transformed into an almost exclusively criminal court.[58] Before October 1551 the court's largest slice of business had concerned unquiet titles to land.[59] In the earlier period it took longer for the real issues in dispute to come to the surface. In the latter part of the sixteenth century there was less justification for further exchange of written argument once the defendant had made his answer and been examined upon interrogatories. When criminal offences were at stake, the facts tended to become apparent more quickly.[60]

As with bills of complaint and answers, replications and rejoinders should be read critically together, and in the context of related research if this is possible, in order that *ex parte* allegations do not result in the drawing of misleading conclusions by the user. The most acceptable pleadings, from the historian's point of view, are those in which basic facts are not disputed, not being at issue between the parties, and the searcher of the pre-1558 Star Chamber records will benefit especially from documents which rehearse details of the successive ownership of land as a prelude to the allegation of an unquiet title.

After the exchange of written pleadings between the parties, the taking of proofs could begin. In practice, testimony began after the filing of the defendant's answer and his own examination. Sworn examinations, which in origin were modelled on the inquisitorial procedures of the ecclesiastical courts,[61] represented the principal way by which the court could establish the facts of cases. Relevant documents, such as charters or leases, were also taken in evidence, but the main emphasis was upon the depositions of witnesses on oath. The oath tendered to witnesses was:

> You shall sweare to make True Answeare to such questions as you shalbe examined upon betweene the parties, and depose the Truth, the whole Trueth and nothing but the Truth without partiality or affeccion to either partie So help you God.[62]

The written interrogatories to be put to the witnesses by the examiner were supplied ready-drawn, having been drafted by counsel in consultation with the party. The number of questions varied. In the early years of Henry VIII's reign, between five and thirty questions was usual; by the 1550s, interrogatories might include up to a hundred separate items. After each witness was produced by the party for whom he appeared, the day on which he was sworn and for which side he appeared were noted. The witness then recited his name, age, profession and dwelling place, the information so useful to genealogists.[63] He then answered the several interrogatories in turn, as tendered by the examiner, and his depositions were formally set out in writing, preserving the phraseology of the questions.[64]

The problem faced by the user of Star Chamber depositions, as it was also by the court itself, is the question of their interpretation. The difficulty arises from the fact that witnesses were privately produced. Thus they were frequently interviewed and coached by their sponsors before they gave evidence, and perjury, subornation, and even straightforward bribery were widespread. Precedents for the punishment in Star Chamber of perjury, committed both in Star Chamber itself and in other courts, especially Chancery, are numerous throughout the sixteenth century.[65] It is clear as a result that proofs must be read as critically as pleadings filed in Star Chamber. In addition to cases of blatant dishonesty, witnesses might be naive, credulous or stupid. They sometimes claimed to have bad memories. A witness might also be honestly mistaken in his impressions, or give a confused account of what had once been a correct impression. All this cuts close indeed to the user of Star Chamber records, especially to the genealogist, since not only is the actual content of the deposition in doubt, but initial statements as to the age, profession and dwelling-place of a witness must be carefully scrutinised.

It has been stated that one-half of the former archive of the court of Star Chamber is missing. For the pre-1558 period, the serious loss is that of the Henrician Council registers, the series of volumes which in 1540 became the Star Chamber order and decree books. In the absence of these books, some detailed knowledge of their form and contents can be derived from manuscripts in the possession of institutions other than the Public Record Office, principally the Huntington Library and the British Library. The chief value of these manuscripts is that they can be used to garner order and decree material copied from records later lost to supplement that which survives in the clerks' papers in STAC 1–4 and STAC 10. Additionally, however, the manuscripts furnish details of suits which passed through the court of Star Chamber for which no proceedings are now extant in the Public Record Office. It has already been noted that even the half of the court's archive which was originally held in the wainscot presses of Star Chamber is now no longer complete. Thus the materials available outside the Public Record Office have a double usefulness to those working on Star Chamber records.

The Ellesmere Manuscripts at the Huntington Library, San Marino, California, contain the papers of Sir Thomas Egerton, lord keeper, and subsequently lord chancellor, from 1596 to 1617. The collection also includes breviates and extracts prepared by the clerical staff of the court of Star

Chamber for the consideration of the chancellor, and a quantity of material of historical interest which belonged to William Mill.[66] The documents are faultlessly preserved in individual folders, and are stored under ideal conditions.[67] The principal manuscripts for the pre-1558 period are the three series of transcripts and extracts from the Council registers, the so-called *Libri Intrationum*. Two of the *Libri*, Ellesmere MSS. 2654 and 2655, were undoubtedly prepared for Sir Thomas Egerton's personal use. He took notes from them, referred to the precedents they contained, and jotted two marginal additions in Ellesmere MS. 2655.[68] Ellesmere MS. 2654 is a handsome book, bound in vellum, and appears to be a fair copy rather than a first attempt. It comprises thirty-two leaves, twenty-five of which contain extracts from the Henrician registers. Ellesmere MS. 2654 is, however, not very useful for the reign of Henry VIII, since all but three folios are devoted to the registers of Henry VII.[69] Ellesmere MS. 2655 concentrates on the years of Wolsey's ascendancy. The manuscript has twenty-two leaves, eighteen of which comprise closely-written extracts from the registers of Henry VII and Henry VIII. Wolsey's chancellorship begins on fo. 9v. and continues to the end of the manuscript. Ellesmere MS. 2655 is unbound, and may once have formed part of a much larger collection of transcripts. It appears to be an original and not a fair copy, and was composed after 1593.[70] Ellesmere MS. 2768, the third *Liber*, forms part of the collection of papers associated with William Mill. It comprises ninety-five leaves, which were formerly part of a larger volume bound in leather.[71] The description *Liber Intrationum* is a misnomer: the manuscript is a disconnected series of transcripts, extracts, precedents, and notes on the antiquity of the court. It was probably begun in 1573, the year in which the younger Mill, while an attorney, acquired the reversion of the clerkship.[72] In 1590 the material was used towards the composition of Mill's 'Discourse concerning the Antiquity of the Star Chamber', and in B. L. Hargrave MS. 216 this treatise is followed by substantial excerpts from the earlier manuscript.[73] The importance of Ellesmere MS. 2768 is the extent to which it utilises the resources of the Henrician Council registers, which were freely available to Mill in his capacity as keeper of the records after 1587. Mill was an eccentric, but he was a vigorous if disorganized researcher. His insatiable appetite for original documents even took him to search the Tower records, where he found 'divers presidents of soe notable a memory for this matter as I assure you the very pleasure of them did recompence my paynes'.[74]

The form of the Council register which covered the greater part of Wolsey's ascendancy is most accurately reproduced by Ellesmere MS. 2655. This manuscript contains the fullest series of Henrician extracts in the Ellesmere collection, and the exact foliation of the original registers has been indicated by the compiler. The extracts for Henry VIII's reign are from the register which ran from the king's accession to 1527. The last entry in Ellesmere MS. 2655 is dated 24 January 1527, by which time 540 folios had been encompassed.[75] The register was completed during 1527, since the inception of the second volume of the reign in that year is recorded in B. L. Lansdowne MS. 160.[76] Egerton's compiler either did not progress to this second register, or his work is not extant.

The authenticity of Ellesmere MS. 2655 can be tested in relation to the surviving official material in the Public Record Office. The extant drafts and copies of the *acta* of the Council in its administrative and judicial capacities confirm that the lay-out of the material in the manuscript represents the usual practice of Richard Eden.[77] Entries were headed by the date in Latin. On the next line was generally written the word *'presentibus'* which was centrally placed. Beneath, a list of the presence, also in Latin, was set out in two parallel columns which flanked the page.[78] If the king were present, the words *'Regia Maiestate'* would appear beneath *'presentibus'*. The left-hand column identified the lords spiritual and other churchmen according to their degrees; the right-hand one listed the names of the lords temporal with their offices, the judges, the knights, and the lawyers. The account of the day's business was then written in the central area. The *acta* of the Council during Wolsey's ascendancy were almost invariably in English.[79]

The method of the compiler of Ellesmere MS. 2655 can also be tested. The entries in the manuscript overlap with eight official drafts of *acta* extant in the Public Record Office. Four official documents contain material parallel to the extracts in Ellesmere MS. 2655. These indicate that the compiler transcribed some original material verbatim. The remainder was paraphrased or abstracted. Wolsey's decree of 11 October 1518 in the case of Dr. John Allen and Sir Christopher Plommer, as recited in Ellesmere MS. 2655, is an almost perfect transcript of the official draft for the Council register.[80] The report of Patrick Bellowe's conduct four days later is, however, a paraphrase:

Ellesmere MS. 2655, fo. 13	Draft for Council register (STAC 2/15/116)
Patricke Bellowe for his obstinacye in refusinge to obaye the decree made yesterdaye betwene him and the Ladye of Slane and the heire of the Boron of Slane late deceased is comitted to the Tower as disobedient to the kinge and his Councell . . .	. . . And for alsmuche as the saide Patricke Bellowe here beyng present in playne co[r]te Refused to obbey the saide decre the same Patrike was comitted to the tower of London as a disobedient subiect to the kinge & his counceile and as a contempno[r] of such Resonable ordres & decres as be made by the king & his saide counceile . . .

The entries for 21 and 25 June 1521, concerning the London grocers, are no more than abstracts of the official version:

Ellesmere MS. 2655, fo. 17

Mr. Norwiche in the name of the hole companye of the grocers confessethe A disobedience in noe better regardinge the kinges Lettres . . .

Draft for Council register (STAC 2/24/50)

. . . First the same wardens & feloushipp by the mouthe of the saide Robert Norwiche sayen confesse & accuse theim selfes that they have offended o^r said soveraign lorde in disobedience for alsmoche as they noo moor humbly & reverently executed his mooste high pleaso^r & comaundementes conteined in his saide most dradd lettres . . .

The other four official documents contain material which should have been included in Ellesmere MS. 2655 had the compiler comprehensively abstracted the business of the sitting days which he chose to record. The entries in Ellesmere MS. 2655 for 2 May 1516, 20 February 1517, 14 October 1518, and 6 November 1518 fail to include the business conducted at the Council board for these days which is recited by the four drafts for the register.[81] The selective nature of the material in Ellesmere MS. 2655 is thus confirmed. The entries in the manuscript give a partial account only of the *acta* of the sitting days cited by the compiler.

While, therefore, Ellesmere MS. 2655 is the most impressive *Liber Intrationum* extant, it is both condensed and selective. The deficiency of material is to some extent remedied by Ellesmere MS. 2652. This manuscript, which is in Sir Thomas Egerton's own hand throughout, comprises twenty-two leaves, three of which are blank.[82] It served as Egerton's personal volume of notes and precedents from the Henrician registers and the later Star Chamber order and decree books for the period 1485–1594. Numbering over seven hundred items, the brief notes of orders and decrees, and points of procedural interest are arranged under headings in roughly chronological order. There are two columns to a page. The headings cover aspects of jurisdiction, process, commissions, affidavits, injunctions, fines and imprisonment, and frivolous suits. A fair proportion of the precedents cover the Henrician period, and the manuscript is useful for the years of Wolsey's ascendancy. As a source of order and decree material, Ellesmere MS. 2652 is of comparable stature to B.L. Harleian MS. 2143, a volume of over six hundred abstracts from the order and decree books.[83]

The remaining manuscripts in the Ellesmere collection which contribute to the historian's knowledge of the Star Chamber archive are the short extracts from the registers prepared by the clerical staff of the Elizabethan court for Sir Thomas Egerton's consideration.[84] Egerton frequently added his own opinions and marginalia, and devised his own short extracts on particular subjects.[85] The matters treated included the court's jurisdiction; the methods of levying fines, costs, and damages; the use of injunctions and commissions; binding to the peace; the punishment of the nobility, and of juries for giving false verdicts; and punishment by exile and banishment.[86] Additional material relating to the clerkship of William Mill provides evidence of the contemporary state of the Star Chamber archive, and the archival habits of the period.[87]

The evidence of the Ellesmere collection at the Huntington Library is supplemented by manuscript material at the British Library. Two *Libri Intrationum* contain matter for the reign of Henry VIII.[88] The more useful of these is B.L. Additional MS. 4521, which comprises forty-eight folios of extracts from the registers of Henry VII and VIII. This *Liber*, which is similar to Ellesmere MS. 2768 as far as 3 June 1508, subsequently continues to 30 January 1545. The additional material consists of twenty Star Chamber decrees, which appear to be verbatim transcripts and cover a five-year span, beginning with the decision of 23 February 1540 in Sir Humphrey Browne's case for giving counsel against the king.[89] It is probable that these decrees were part of a further series of extracts from the court's order and decree books. Other versions of the same twenty decrees are extant, but all the available manuscripts are copies, and the provenance of the decrees remains uncertain.[90]

More substantial is the series of extracts and transcripts made by William Hudson from the Henrician registers and Star Chamber order and decree books towards the end of the second decade of the seventeenth century.[91] The work was in preparation for Hudson's scholarly treatise on the court.[92] The extracts are extant in the form of a copy by John Lightfoot, contained in B.L. Lansdowne MS. 639. They are introduced by the marginal note: 'Here begin the Mate[r]s Copied out of M[r] Hudsons Booke And they continue till Pag. 217. 10. Junii 1636. J[ohn] L[ightfoot]'.[93] A memorandum by Lightfoot of the same date, included towards the end of the extracts, records that: 'Note here that by the word [My] is meant William Hudson esq[r] an ancient practiser and most & best experienced Councellor attending this Court, my Patron, the Composer and Collecto[r] of the Matte[r]s contayned in this Booke'.[94] Hudson's notes for his treatise, which cover the period 1494–1618, now occupy eighty-eight folios of manuscript. Comparison of the notes with three surviving official drafts for the register which contain parallel matter, and with Ellesmere MS. 2655, establishes that Hudson's extracts were derived directly from the originals.[95] Most of the extracts appear to be paraphrases or abstracts. Lightfoot seems to have copied the notes as he found them, although, judging from a number of mis-spellings which are scattered through the manuscript, he may have found Hudson's hand difficult at times. The extracts are particularly comprehensive for the period 1509–1517; thereafter, the amount of detail given is less substantial, and it looks as if Hudson's enthusiasm for original research waned when faced with the bulk of Henry VIII's first Council register. The material is, however, more than satisfactory for the years before 1529.[96]

Hudson's Star Chamber notes comprise interlocutory orders and final decrees, orders for writs of *subpoena* and privy seal summonses, orders for commissions of *dedimus potestatem*, entries of appearances, admissions to attorney, affidavits, recognisances for appearance and for good behaviour, injunctions, and committals for contempt. Transcripts and abstracts from the purely administrative *acta* of the Council are also included.[97] Much of the documentation is not otherwise extant, and a small proportion supplements the Star Chamber proceedings, enabling the pleadings and proofs of individual suits to be matched with eventual orders and decrees or related information. A few Henrician extracts carry a list of the presence, which flanks the text, but the lay-out of most of the material bears no resemblance to what is known of the original registers.[98] Many of the extracts are undated and are run together in a way which would be confusing were it not for the familiarity of some of the material. The added regnal years, apparently supplied by Lightfoot, are inaccurate. The brief notes in Ellesmere MS. 2652 supply some otherwise unknown dates; Sir Thomas Egerton was more methodical than most other collectors of precedents. Also the folios of Hudson's notebook may have been disordered at the time that Lightfoot began work, since the material is not entirely in chronological order, and the reign of Henry VIII is interrupted by abstracts of cases of 1557 and 1604.[99] B.L. Lansdowne MS. 639 is nevertheless of secondary importance only to the *Libri Intrationum* in the Ellesmere collection as a source for the reconstruction of something of the contents of the Council registers which covered the fourteen years of Wolsey's ascendancy.

Further extracts from the lost Henrician Council registers and Star Chamber order and decree books are located in other manuscripts among the collections at the British Library. The most important of these is Harleian MS. 2143 containing six hundred abstracts from the order and decree books for the period 1552–1596. As a source of order and decree material, Harleian MS. 2143 is of comparable stature to Ellesmere MS. 2652. When combined, these two manuscripts provide evidence of the outcome of rather more than a thousand sixteenth-century cases, and enable large numbers of extant Star Chamber Proceedings in the classes STAC 1–4 and STAC 10 to be matched with an eventual result. Only the estreats of fines to be found for the reign of Elizabeth on the Memoranda Rolls of the Exchequer, King's Remembrancer, in the Public Record Office yield a more effective method of determining the outcome of suits.[100] Such evidence is, however, unavailable for the Henrician and Edwardian period, though it begins in Mary's reign since the process by which fines were paid and accounted for according to the course of the

Exchequer was linked to the transformation of Star Chamber into an exclusively criminal court.[101] The remaining manuscripts at the British Library which offer the user of the pre-1558 Star Chamber records material otherwise unobtainable are Lansdowne MSS. 1 and 160; Harleian MSS. 305 and 425; and Cotton MSS. Vespasian C. xiv and Vespasian F. xiii. The most useful contribution offered by these items is the series of extracts in Lansdowne MS. 160 entitled: 'Notes out of the star chamber books temporibus H.7. et H.8. touching those who sat then there as Judges'.[102] These extracts, by their content and appearance, were undoubtedly taken from the lost volumes last heard of in the Star Chamber office and the house in St. Bartholomew's Close, London.

CHAPTER THREE
Star Chamber Procedure to 1558

Private suits in the court of Star Chamber were initiated by the filing of a bill of complaint.[1] The English bill, throughout its development, retained the ancient format of the petition from which it was derived: the tone was that of supplication on the part of the 'loyal subject' and 'humble orator', and ritual prayers for the health and longevity of the sovereign were included beside the charges against the defendant.[2] As an alternative pleading to the bill of complaint, and apart from the suits of the attorney-general and the king's almoner, an information by a private individual might set litigation in progress. In theory, the distinction between the bill and the information was that the bill was appropriate when an individual was himself the aggrieved party, and the information when some wrong done to the crown was alleged. Informations of this type usually described themselves as 'for the king's advantage', and were adopted mainly in cases of officers' malfeasance, or intrusions on the king's possession.[3] However, in practice the distinction was not maintained. Individuals exhibited informations on purely private matters, and these were acceptable to the court.[4]

Official or government prosecutions in Star Chamber – there were few before 1540 – were initiated by the attorney-general. In theory, the king's suits were not bound by the strict rules of procedure but only by the order which the court should make. Nevertheless, the normal practice was the filing of a written information.[5] In response the defendant either answered the charges in the usual way or admitted his offence and signed a confession. Although the attorney-general did sometimes present his case *ore tenus*, this was exceptional; moreover, subsequent proceedings continued by the method only if the defendant was willing to sign a confession.[6] Similarly, the king's almoner's suits for the king's alms almost invariably began by bill. In and after the 1530s, it was accepted that the almoner should proceed in Star Chamber against a person or persons suspected of withholding the goods of a *felo de se* or deodands.[7] Theoretically, the almoner, like the attorney-general, was not tied to any strict rule of prosecution, but he normally adhered to the course of the court.

It should, however, be noted that the ancient rule that suits were initiated by bill was often honoured more in the breach than in the observance. Sixteenth-century practice increasingly permitted the issue of process before the filing of the written bill or information.[8] Although condemned from time to time by such rigorous lord chancellors as Sir Thomas More or Sir Thomas

Egerton, the system had come to recognise that the writ of *subpoena* issued as a matter of course.[9] The detrimental aspect of the practice was that the plaintiff need not have finalized nor in any way committed himself to his accusation when process was issued. A related development provided that if the plaintiff had indeed filed a bill of complaint at the time of suing out of process, he would be allowed to amend his bill or to substitute a new one up to the day scheduled for the return of his process.[10] However, amendment was not possible after the defendant had entered his appearance. If process had been issued before the bill was exhibited, the plaintiff had to perfect and file his bill by the time of the defendant's appearance. Should he fail to file a bill, the defendant would secure his dismissal with costs.[11] In cases where the bill was ruled insufficient, the defendant again obtained dismissal with costs.[12] As a deterrent against frivolous suits, lord chancellors ultimately relied on the pillory, the Fleet or a flogging.[13]

The original process of the court of Star Chamber was the writ *quibusdam certis de causis*. In the reign of Henry VII, it took the form of a summons issued in English under the privy seal.[14] It did not necessarily specify the cause of summons, had a penalty clause inserted of £40 upwards, and was not returnable. This form of process continued into the reign of Henry VIII, and an isolated example may be found as late as the reign of Edward VI.[15] The penalty was increased to £100, although it might be as much as £500. However, the form of process which came to be preferred in and after Wolsey's ascendancy was the writ of *subpoena*.[16] In this form, the *quibusdam certis de causis* was issued in Latin under the great seal, had the *subpoena* clause inserted, and was returnable. The penalty was uniformly £100, and £200 or £500 in notorious criminal cases. The writ was correctly described as the *subpoena ad comparendum*.[17]

Process summoned the defendants to appear in person by a fixed day of return. Star Chamber organized its business according to the law terms, and the return days were those set for the common law courts.[18] In serious criminal cases, the defendant might be ordered to appear immediately on receipt of the writ or within a week, or on pain of allegiance, but these instances were exceptional. The penalty specified in the writ was not itself enforceable, as was the case with Chancery writs of *subpoena*, being *in terrorem tantum*; but if the defendant disobeyed the original writ, he would on his subsequent appearance by process of contempt be bound in a recognisance to his future appearance. Should he fail to keep this, the penalty of the recognisance would be forfeit and leviable by the course of the Exchequer.[19]

Privy seal summonses and writs of *subpoena* appear to have been reasonably effective. The methods employed in the face of disobedience and non-appearance by defendants were attachment, followed by attachment with proclamation, and finally commission of rebellion.[20] When the defendant presented himself in court, the clerk of the Council in Star Chamber would make the entry of his appearance in his register.[21] The defendant was then obliged to exhibit his answer to the plaintiff's bill of complaint, and would be sworn and examined as to the truth of his statement.[22] The answer was then filed. Defendants who hesitated or delayed would be commanded by the court to answer and be sworn.[23] It was, however, possible to plead to the jurisdiction of the court prior to answering.[24] There were few instances of the filing of demurrers prior to Mary's reign; nevertheless some defendants attempted to combine special pleading and a challenge to the jurisdiction of the court with an answer.[25] Thus in cases which included allegations of extreme violence resulting in death, the defendant, before going on to answer, might claim that the bill was only determinable at common law because it touched life and limb.[26] By the 1550s, the demurrer existed as a separate instrument in Star Chamber; but the Tudor court generally remained hostile to demurrers 'for that it is an offence to the Jurisdiccion of the Courte to demurre, and Costes putt uppon him that doth demurre, yf it be ruled against him'.[27]

Answer was exhibited on oath.[28] Contrary to Chancery practice, the defendant was then examined in court on any questions of fact arising. Before about 1520 there was usually only one stage: the defendant, having been sworn, went on to make a short declaration. This statement was usually brief and was endorsed on the answer, although if it was longer a separate sheet of paper was used.[29] The procedure was at an elementary stage. Later in Henry VIII's reign, a more developed form for the examination of defendants may be observed. There might be two stages. The defendant first swore that his written answer was true. Then, if the plaintiff had filed written interrogatories for use in the examination, the questions were put to the defendant while he was still on oath, and the answers he gave were written down on paper by a clerk of the Council.[30] The procedure followed would vary in length in each case: the court possessed discretionary powers to examine defendants as was necessary.[31]

If, after the defendant's examination, the court was persuaded that he was the victim of a frivolous suit, he would be discharged from further appearance. However, such dismissals were not often possible and the court had to be on constant alert for perjury. Should perjury be discovered in the examination, the defendant would be punished by the pillory, the wearing of humiliating papers in Westminster Hall and his home locality, or by imprisonment in the Fleet.[32] The same applied to perjury by witnesses in their examinations. The early Star Chamber was always prepared to punish perjury summarily, irrespective of whether or not it had been complained of by bill or information.[33]

For the defendant to be sworn on his answer in court, he had to appear in person. If for a reason acceptable to the court he could not make his appearance, the court – after sworn affidavit by his representative – would appoint a commission to receive the answer in the locality under authority of a writ of *dedimus potestatem*.[34] Early in Henry VIII's reign, these commissions were awarded after affidavit made in open court. By the 1530s, however, a clerk of the Council made the necessary arrangements out of court. Acceptable reasons, for the purpose of a commission, were generally ill-health or indisposition.[35] The commission *ad recipiendum responsionem* would be attached to the bill of complaint itself or to a copy-bill. The writ instructed the commissioners to take the defendant's answer in his locality, to swear and examine the defendant on the subject-matter of the bill, and to make certificate in writing of the same generally by a stated date in the following term.[36] A certificate returned to Star Chamber in Mary's reign makes clear that the procedure was still in force:

> Pleasythe it your most excellent Majesties to be advertysed, That we accordinge to the Tenor and purporte of your most gracious wryte to us directid have Repaired to the within namyd Richard Butler and William Brecknocke beyng old and aged men, And them have examyned upon the bill of complainte of Edward Kyneston to your highnes exhibited. And have Receaved Their Answere beynge sworne befor us upon th'olie evangelist, which answere we have sent herein enclosed annexid to the said writt and bill of complaint for further order therein to be takyn by your highnes And your most honorable Counsaill accordinge to our bounden dutie.[37]

In the reign of Henry VII, it had been the Council's policy to extend the terms of commissions *ad recipiendum responsionem* to include also the commission *ad audiendum et examinandum testes*, by virtue of which the examination of witnesses as well as defendants might be effected in the locality.[38] This would further aid the defendant's conduct of his case, while perhaps expediting the suit and avoiding expense to both parties. The practice continued in the reign of Henry VIII. Simultaneously the court encouraged parties to civil litigation to join in commission for the final determination of their cases in the country.[39] This method of procedure was well established by 1525: commissions *ad audiendum et finaliter determinandum* issued without any special circumstances if both sides consented to the arrangement. The rationale was essentially that of mediation and arbitration rather than determination.[40] Yet most of these commissions to hear and end were abortive and the cases resumed at London.[41]

As Star Chamber became transformed into an almost exclusively criminal court in the early years of Elizabeth's reign, commissions *ad audiendum et finaliter determinandum* withered away.[42] Such commissions could not be adapted to truly criminal business: after about 1560 writs of *dedimus potestatem* were only granted either to examine defendants or witnesses upon interrogatories in the country. Elaborate rules for examinations of defendants were correspondingly evolved by the court:

> If the plaintiff shall neglect to exhibit his Articles at the execucion of the Commis-

sion the same being duly sued out and executed, the defendant shall not be after-wards compelled to any further examinacion, but the plaintiff [is] to loose the benefit thereof, without speciall Order of the Court therein.

If a defendant returne his answeare upon dedimus potestatem without any examina-cion upon Interr[ogatorie]s, an attachment shalbe awarded against him unles hee make it appeare by affidavit or Certificat that the plaintiff did minister noe Interr[ogatorie]s.[43]

When the defendant appeared in person before the court to file his answer and was sworn and examined, depending on the nature of the case and the court's discretion, he might be admitted to attorney and licensed to depart, or required to make future appearances in person.[44] In Henry VII's reign and early in his son's, admissions to attorney were not a matter of course: an order of the court was required to discharge each defendant of his personal attendance.[45] Suits in Star Chamber were on first sight criminal or quasi-criminal and in consequence defendants would be enjoined to make them-selves available, and not to depart without the licence of the court. Eventual-ly, increasing business and resultant delays made it necessary to recognise the true situation. The majority of pre-1558 suits were in fact essentially civil in character and concerned title to real property.[46] It was Wolsey who made the crucial decision: on 5 February 1527, he announced that those defendants accused of riot who denied in their answers that they had used violence should be admitted to attorney automatically and licensed to depart.[47] On 21 May the same year the ruling was confirmed: 'it is ordered that all such persons as be brought up hither by bill and in theire Answers to the same billes doe confesse noe riott . . . shall be admitted to the Attorney'.[48] The clerk of the Council was to effect such admissions to attorney without further reference to the lord chancellor or the court.

In the attorney-general's suits, in genuine criminal suits brought by private parties, and in cases where the defendant had offered disobedience or con-tempt, the conditions of personal appearance remained as they had been in the reign of Henry VII. The daily attendance of the defendant throughout the legal term might be required – and frequently was.[49] In these instances, the defendant was ordered to enter into a recognisance for his daily appearance and good behaviour in sums which varied from £100 to £1000. Defendants were often obliged to provide security for the peace, and additional sureties could be required who entered into parallel recognisances in £40 upwards.[50] Defendants might even be required to pay into court the sum required as security for the peace in cash or plate.[51] Those defendants in criminal cases who had been imprisoned in the Fleet after answer and examination would on completion of these formalities be discharged under the conditions of their recognisances. Those who were rash enough to fail in their daily appearances would be committed to prison for contempt, and the penalties of their recog-nisances would be forfeit and leviable.[52]

The second stage in the exchange of written pleadings was that of replication and rejoinder. It seems from the beginning that where (in a minority of cases) the defendant in his answer pleaded 'not guilty' to the charges against him, replication and therefore rejoinder might be omitted. The plea of 'not guilty' did not touch the factual allegation of the bill and put the matter averred at issue between the parties.[53] The omission of replication and rejoinder was less usual after the reign of Henry VIII: defendants were required to state their version of the truth and matters of fact invariably arose which demanded challenge. There were normally also counter-allegations to which the plaintiff had to reply. The mature court of Star Chamber was, however, strict upon its interpretation of a defence plea of 'not guilty':

> If the defendants plead generally not guiltie to the whole Bill, the plaintiff shall not Reply at all. And noe Replicacion is to be received where all the defendants plead generally Not guiltie, for it is a meere delay they being allreadie at issue upon not guiltie. If a defendant do answeare specially to the whole Bill or some partes thereof and shall afterwards plead not guiltie generally, the same shall not be taken as a generall not guiltie, but the plaintiff shall have libertie to reply to the speciall Answeare.[54]

Yet if a replication was required in reply to a defendant's answer, a case could be dismissed with costs should the plaintiff fail to provide one.[55] The plaintiff could not be compelled to reply until all his opponents had filed their answers and been examined upon interrogatories,[56] but when they had, compulsion increasingly became the order of the day. For as Star Chamber litigation became primarily collateral and strategic after 1558, the precise timing of replication or rejoinder by parties was linked to the progress of their related suits in other courts. Star Chamber was thus obliged to evolve complex rules to ensure fair play and counter dilatory proceedings by scheming litigants. If plaintiffs did not file their replications by the time appointed by the court, they faced dismissal with costs. In turn, they were permitted from Elizabeth's reign onwards to obtain writs of *subpoena ad reiungendum* to compel defendants to rejoin to the replication within a set time.[57]

The defendant's rejoinder was designed to counteract the plaintiff's replication. In the mature Star Chamber, the defendant was not obliged to rejoin until he had been served with process *ad reiungendum*,[58] but under Henry VIII it does not seem that any pressure could be brought to encourage a defendant to rejoin save by special order of the court. If a replication had been filed, a rejoinder was essential to the progress of a suit, since otherwise the parties could not come to an issue.[59] However, plaintiffs in the post-1558 Star Chamber were permitted to begin the taking of testimony from witnesses in the period pending the dilatory defendant's replication.[60] Very rarely after the replication was filed, the plaintiff might continue the argument by exhibiting a surrejoinder to challenge the factual content of the defendant's rejoinder.[61]

After the exchange of written pleadings between the parties, the taking of proofs could begin in earnest. In the reign of Henry VII, a procedure for the examination of witnesses was in a stage of incipient development. The parties produced their witnesses and sometimes supplied interrogatories ready-drawn for the examination of specified witnesses. The questions were put by an examiner who was either a councillor or the clerk of the Council, and the depositions were taken in open court, being recorded in a continuous narrative.[62] The origins of these arrangements may be traced from the time when the King's Council, after receiving a written petition, might conduct the entire case *viva voce*. By 1558, however, the court's mature procedure had become settled in all its important aspects.

Although Star Chamber depositions were taken initially in open court, by 1530 they had moved out of court. A councillor or, more usually, one of the clerks of the Council acted as examiner.[63] If councillors were officiating as examiners, a clerk acted as secretary. Day would be given to the party to produce his witnesses for questioning; the witnesses then appeared by arrangement with their sponsors, who guaranteed their expenses, and in most cases suitably charged them as to the evidence they should give. If an essential witness refused to attend, a privy seal summons or writ of *subpoena ad testificandum* would be issued against him.[64] Examinations were conducted in secret, and the depositions taken were kept secret until the court ordered publication. Depositions taken after publication were invalid, save in exceptional cases when additional examinations were ordered by the court pending or during judgment.[65] Both sides conducted separate examinations, and a witness might not be examined more than once on each side. Witnesses could, however, be cross-examined later by either side.[66]

As an alternative to the taking of proofs in London, parties might obtain the permission of the court to join in commission for the examination of witnesses in the locality, the commissioners acting under the authority of a writ of *dedimus potestatem*.[67] By the 1530s, the opportunity to join in commission for the taking of proofs became available to litigants without limitation to cases of ill-health and indisposition. Under pressure of business, the court was willing to issue commissions *ad audiendum et examinandum testes* without special circumstances. The clerk of the Council prepared the warrant for the writ at the request of the parties; when the writ issued, it was attached to a sheet of parchment upon which the pleadings previously exhibited by the respective parties had been copied.[68] Interrogatories might also be supplied for the use of the commissioners. The writ instructed the commissioners to swear the witnesses, examine them and record their answers. The depositions were to be engrossed on parchment and returned to the court under seal by a stated day of return. By 1540, interrogatories supplied ready-drawn were an essential part of the procedure, and strict differentiation was observed between commissions of *dedimus potestatem ad recipiendum responsionem* and *ad audiendum et examinandum testes*.[69]

The procedures by which evidence was taken before commissioners in the localities can be seen in operation in an enclosure case of the reign of Edward VI.[70] The suit, *Darcy* v. *Tempest et al.*, concerned the allegedly illegal enclosure of common land on the manor of Guisborough in the North Riding of Yorkshire. After the plaintiff's replication, a writ of *dedimus potestatem* was issued in English to four local gentry:

> Edward the sixt by the grace of God kyng of England, Fraunce and Ireland, defendour of the faythe and of the churche of England, and also of Ireland in erthe the supreme hedd. To our trustie and welbeloved William Vavasour knight, Robert Menyell serieaunt at lawe, Robert Chalonor and George Browne Esquyers, gretyng. Knowe ye that we of th'especyall trust and confydence that wee have in your circumspect and approved wysdoms have assigned you foure, three or twoe of you, and by vertue hereof do gyve unto you foure, three or twoe of you full power and auctorytie to surveye and vew the gronde nowe in varyance and controversye betwene Sir Arthure Darcy knight playntyf, and Sir John Tempest knight and other defendauntes, and to make a true plat [map] therof and to take order for the commen theron according to the accoustomed usage therof, and also to here all maner of wytnes before you to be brought aswell on the parties plaintyf as on the parties defendauntes apon certeyn interrogatories herein enclosed, and the same wytnes and every of theym dylygently to examyn by all the wayes and meanes as ye shall thinke requisyte and necessarie apon ther othes. And the examinacions of them to take and put in wryting. And when ye have this our present commaundement executed, we wyll that ye certifie us and our Counsell in the sterr chamber at Westminster in the quindezim of Easter next commyng under your sealles or the sealles of you foure, three or two of you distynctly and playnly what you have done heryn, sending unto us the interrogatories aforesaid with this our wrytt, furthermore enyonyng the parties above named in our behalf to observe and kepe our peace untill suche tyme as we and our Counsell have made fynall end betwene them concernyng the premisses. Wytnes our self at Westminster the xvij day of Novembre the thyrd yere of our reygne.
>
> Smyth[71]

Before the dissolution of the monasteries, Star Chamber commissions tended to conjoin the local leaders of church and state in the task of collecting evidence and taking examinations of witnesses upon the interrogatories supplied by parties. After 1540, however, the court relied on the responsibility of the laity, especially on landed gentlemen and those lawyers who resided out of term in the provinces. The inclusion of at least one qualified common lawyer in each Star Chamber commission was normal from Sir Thomas Audley's chancellorship onwards. This custom reflected the enhanced professionalism, settled procedure, and burgeoning awareness of a sense of precedent that characterised the court after the streamlining of the 1530s.

The mature Star Chamber recognized certain fixed rules for the selection of commissioners to take evidence. Parties were not to propose as commissioners those near to them in consanguinity or affinity, those who had been retained as barristers, attorneys or solicitors in connection with the suit, those who were their tenants or landlords, nor anyone who was regarded as their master or servant, patron or client. In addition, persons with a personal interest in the outcome of a suit, or who were themselves engaged in litigation with the other side were not to be named to the commission.[72]

After the examination of witnesses was completed, the depositions were placed on the public file and the parties and their attorneys were permitted to take copies in order that each side might prepare its case for the hearing. A motion for final hearing was then made, by party or attorney, and a day was set by the court for determination.[73] Cases might come to hearing in two ways: after the exchange of written pleadings and the taking of proofs, or after a sworn confession made by the defendant. Familiar procedures of litigation were curtailed normally only in the suits of the attorney-general, either in cases of political importance, when the accused feared incurring royal displeasure by denying his offence, or when defendants and their advisers had secured an advantage by plea-bargaining or had hopes of remission of sentence by a royal pardon.[74] If any of the parties was out of town, his attorney had the duty of informing him when publication had passed and the day for the hearing had been fixed. A party might then set out for London to instruct his counsel and to appear in court. From the 1530s onwards, a writ of *subpoena ad audiendum iudicium* could be obtained to compel a reluctant opponent to complete outstanding business by attending the hearing of his case.[75] If, on the other hand, the defendant appeared for the hearing on time, but the plaintiff procrastinated or was not ready, the defendant was awarded his costs.[76]

Hearing and judgment of suits at Westminster was in open court before the lord chancellor and the Council assembled in the outer Star Chamber. After the creation of the Privy Council, the bench usually comprised the reformed Council plus the chief justices and the chief baron of the Exchequer (and sometimes selected puisne justices). At the opening of the hearing counsel for the plaintiff recited the bill of complaint, and counsel for the defendant replied by reading the answer. Long pleadings were summarized rather than read verbatim. Any points which had emerged in later pleadings were stated, and extracts from the depositions of the witnesses and any other relevant documents, especially title-deeds or leases, were read to the court.[77] Counsel then summed up their respective cases. If the suit was to be determined, the chancellor and the Council would deliberate amongst themselves and then, calling the counsel of the parties before them, give judgment.[78]

In criminal cases there was rarely any need before 1558 to delay. Judgment and sentence would swiftly follow the hearing and debating of the salient issues. Star Chamber was not yet the forum for expounding legal theory and making new law by judicial pronouncement that it became in the later years of Elizabeth I.[79] In the pre-1558 period, criminal cases in the court were decided on the facts in accordance with existing criminal law and the Council's inherent jurisdiction to punish wrongdoing. The defendant would be sentenced to fine, imprisonment or some form of corporal punishment.[80]

Thus on 13 July 1518 John Vesacreley was sentenced after the hearing of a case brought by a plaintiff from whom he had fraudulently gained four marks:

> It is decreed that the same John Vesacreley shalbe immediatlye convayed to the Fleete there to remayne till to morrowe. And then in the morninge at Markett tyme to be convayed to London by the warden of the Fleete or his deputye, and there to be delivered to the Sheriffes by whom yt is decreed that the same John Vesacreley shalbe sett uppon the Pillorye with a large paper uppon his head wherin shalbe wrytten in greate lettres 'This man hathe committed extorcion'.[81]

The defendant was then to remain incarcerated in the Fleet until the four marks were repaid to the plaintiff.

In 1530 Sir Thomas More, as chancellor, sent Agnes Curwen from Star Chamber to the cucking stool for falsely claiming that Sir Humfrey Conyngesby, secondary justice of King's Bench, had accepted for engrossment the text of a final concord concerning her lands which she had not acknowledged. The woman was to be fastened to the stool and dipped three times into the Thames on ropes from Westminster bridge.[82] It is probable that this was one of a number of summary sentences handed down in Henry VIII's reign for slanderous words against the judiciary. On 8 February 1537 Richard Vowles was ordered by Star Chamber to the pillory and to lose both his ears 'for that he foolishelie, lewdelie and sclaunderouselie like a seditious and lighte person made complainte to the kinges highnes by bill of his owne hande uppon James Fitzjames, chiefe Justice of Englande, and the cause therein not proved'.[83] In April 1544 Richard Whittingestall was 'committed to the Fleete and Pillorie for false accusation and sclaunderous exclamacion made uppon the Recorder of London'.[84]

The corporal punishments for which Star Chamber became notorious, and which were received into regular usage after *Vowles's Case*, culminating in 1634 in *Prynne's Case*,[85] were perhaps borrowed from those inflicted by the lay power in the thirteenth century on persons convicted in the ecclesiastical courts of the sin of blasphemy.[86] In addition to the cropping of ears, the early Star Chamber sentenced defendants to have their ears nailed to the pillory and to public floggings.[87] In Michaelmas term 1556 a man was ordered to be branded with a hot iron upon both cheeks with the letters 'F' and 'A' to signify 'False Accusation', after which he was to be sent to the pillory for two days each at Ipswich and Norwich. But he was first to wear papers advertising his offence at Westminster, riding on horseback but facing the animal's tail.[88]

Fines imposed by the pre-1558 Star Chamber ranged from 20 shillings to

1000 marks. The £6000 fine imposed on Lord Paget in June 1552 was exceptional, the case being political and the amount *in terrorem tantum*.[89] In Hilary term 1517 Thomas Trentham paid £5 for contempt, Sir Walter Calverley was fined £10 for riot and £10 for contempt, and John Copinger's fine for abduction was assessed at 100 marks.[90] In November 1518 Sir William Brereton indented for a fine of 500 marks for 'comforting' felons.[91] But fines had increased by mid-century. In Easter term 1553 Sir John Southworth was fined £500 for riot, killing cattle, perjury, and disobeying an injunction. He was bound in a recognisance in the sum of £1000 to pay his fine, together with damages and costs to the plaintiff. His servants were to stand on the pillory.[92] When Southworth failed to pay his fine, he was sent to the Fleet prison.[93] A year later, in Easter term 1554, each member of a London jury was fined 1000 marks for acquitting Sir Nicholas Throckmorton of treason contrary to the attorney-general's evidence that he had been implicated in Wyatt's rebellion.[94] In addition, two of the jurors were sent to the Tower for 'slanderous words' in saying that they were as true men as ever departed from Star Chamber. Other fines imposed in Mary's reign included £6 13s. 4d. for allowing a heretic to escape from prison, sums ranging from £5 to 300 marks for riot plus costs and damages, £10 for maintenance, £200 for perjury, and £100 and 100 marks for illegal export of herrings.[95] However, fines in Mary's reign were sometimes linked to the ability of the offender to pay. One defendant was sent to the Fleet and fined 'but at £10 for his poverty'.[96]

Yet criminal cases were in a minority in Star Chamber before 1558. The majority of suits prior to the change in the court's direction about 1560 were disputes concerning real or personal property, and litigation invariably turned on the respective titles of the parties in such cases.[97] This does not mean that property was not at the bottom of many suits in the Elizabethan or Jacobean Star Chamber. On the contrary, four-fifths of all cases in the Jacobean court had property either at stake or in some way connected with the action. After the jurisdictional transformation of Star Chamber in Elizabeth's reign, essentially civil ends were necessarily clad in criminal raiment.[98] Before 1558 lord chancellors pursued individual policies: they had their own ideas as to the procedure by which real property suits should be tackled in Chancery, Star Chamber and the other English bill courts. The basic practice in Star Chamber, however, which Wolsey established and his successors retained, was that the points at issue, having been identified, would be referred either to legal experts for adjudication and report, or to arbitrators or mediators for solution by compromise between the parties.[99] Whatever decision was finally proposed would be reviewed by the court and, if approved, would be made the basis of a final decree.[100]

Under pressure of business, the pre-1558 Star Chamber attempted to refer real property disputes for settlement in the country by the arbitration and mediation of local persons of credit. As late as Mary's reign, the court regularly allowed parties to join in commission after the plaintiff's replication for the hearing of their cases in the country without special circumstances.[101] These commissions of *dedimus potestatem ad audiendum et finaliter determinandum* were addressed to landed gentry or other persons of status, who were often justices of the peace. They had local knowledge and social authority; the court, while attempting to reduce the arrears of work at the centre, was optimistic that disputes might be swiftly ended if the parties could be brought together under supervision to iron out their differences. Commissions issued with the consent of the parties, who generally themselves suggested the names of commissioners to the court. A few *ex parte* commissions were also awarded, but these seem to have been confined to early cases where the plaintiff from the start preferred the mediation of local gentlemen to the summoning of the defendant to London.[102] When the writ of *dedimus potestatem* issued, it ordered the commissioners to hear and examine the matters in variance between the parties, and to reach a peaceful end if they could or else to certify the court by a fixed date usually in the following term. The commission was attached to the bill of complaint, or a copy-bill, and any subsequent pleadings or other material necessary to the success of the inquiry would be engrossed on parchment and sent in addition. The commissioners were to return the matter sent to them when they despatched the certificate of what they had done. This certificate was to be in writing under their respective seals and was to be engrossed on parchment.[103]

As a procedure for the settlement of litigation, commissions to hear and end appear consistently to have been ineffective. Commissioners, after considering the allegations and claims of both sides and after calling witnesses before them, tended to certify to similar effect:

> For asmoche as we betwen the same parties could make none fynall determynacion in the matter in varyaunce dependyng betwen theym, we therfor accordyng to the tenor of the same commyssyon do send onto your grace and oder lordes of the kinges most honorable Counsaill the byll of Complaynt and th'answer and the said deposycions with the said Commyssyon in this our certificat inclosed assigned and sealyd with our handes.[104]

This lack of success was not the result of the incompetence or procrastination of the commissioners. The procedure to be followed was clear and familiar, and those appointed were disciplined in such matters. Even after Audley's reform whereby the court always mixed professional lawyers with the other commissioners, the result was equally abortive. The lord chancellor might sometimes have to galvanize commissioners into activity, but these cases were exceptional.[105] It was the conduct of the litigants themselves that was the prime cause of failure. If a party perceived that the commissioners were against him, he would obstruct proceedings and desire remission to London. If he saw from the evidence that he had the weaker case, he would withdraw co-operation and demand remission to the common law. Most frequently, commissioners were unable to mediate because the parties were stubborn and refused to agree on a settlement. In these circumstances, a case would be referred back to Westminster, the commissioners generally giving the parties their day of appearance in Star Chamber, and informing the court of the same in their certificate.[106]

When a case did eventually reach its conclusion, either by judgment delivered in court, reference, arbitration or compromise, the decision was pronounced in the form of a decree. Final decrees were dictated by the lord chancellor and were published as being enacted and adjudged by him and the other lords of the king's most honourable Council.[107] The authority behind the decree was always that of the lord chancellor and King's Council, irrespective of precisely how the determination of a particular suit had been achieved. The decree was then entered into the current register of Star Chamber by the clerk of the Council there. Copies of decrees were issued to the parties; where necessary, an applicant could also obtain an exemplification under the great seal.[108]

The cautious phraseology of some of the civil decrees which remain extant suggests that the court contemplated varying degrees of finality in making its decrees, according to the circumstances of a case at the point of determination. Some decrees did not exclude the possibility of further order, or awarded possession of land to a party with the proviso that the other party might initiate new proceedings at common law.[109] Even a decree describing itself as 'final' might later on hold out the prospect of review in the light of new evidence. Such a decree was pronounced in 1526 in *Payne* v. *Lambert*:

In camera stellata nono die februarij anno regni regis henrici octavi decimo septimo

Memorandum that in the terme of sainte hillary in the xvij[th] yere of the reigne of our soveraigne lorde Henry the viij[th] . . . yt ys . . . finally decreed and adiudged by the said moste Reverent fader in god and oder the said moste honorable councell in the said Sterre chambre att Westminster the [ninth] day of February in the said xvij[th] yere of the Reigne of our said soveraigne lorde kinge Henry the viij[th] that the said John Payne shall entre into the said mese and landes with th'appurtenaunces and the same to have and enioye to hym and hys heires. And that the said Henry Lambert shall permitte and suffer the said John Payne to entre into the same mese and landes with th'appurtenaunces and the same to have, occupie and enioye to hys and theire propre use without lett, interupcion or disturbaunce of the said Henry Lambert or of his heires, or any oder person or persons by his or theire procurement, abetment, commaundement or means, untyll suche tyme that it shall appere or be dewly and substanceally proved by the said Henry or his heires by evidens, witnes or oderwise in the same Sterre chambre before the Chauncelor of Englonde for the tyme beinge and the lordes and oder the kinges moste honorable councell for the tyme being that the said Henry Lambert hath better right and title aswell in Constiens as in lawe and good equite to the premisses then the said John Payne hath. So and in such wyse that the same proofe shalbe by the Chauncelor, lordes and oder of the kinges moste honorable counsell for the tyme beinge in the said

Sterre chambre accepted, taken and by theym decreed for the same Henry that he hath better title in Constiens, lawe and good equite to the premisses then the said Payne hath.[110]

Yet unlike this example, a few civil decrees were emphatic as to their finality. They repudiated any suggestion that the judgment could be reversed, and demanded that the unsuccessful party 'sease and relynquysse all suche feynyd and untrewe accions and sutes as he . . . hath commensed and takyn . . . in any Court of our Sovereigne lorde the kyng within the Realme of England' upon the matter in question.[111]

Successful litigants in civil suits were usually awarded costs.[112] Many applied for damages, too, which were steadily awarded as the sixteenth century progressed.[113] In a very real sense the decision to offer damages made Star Chamber's fortune. The prospect of winning cash compensation, in addition to some coveted prize in relation to a property matter, guaranteed the court's later popularity. Yet a favourable decree was not always the same as satisfaction, and Star Chamber had a poor record in terms of the finality of its decrees in civil suits before 1558. The court was not oblivious, however, to the problem of enforcement.[114] The methods adopted to secure compliance were penal recognisances, which bound defeated parties to observe the court's decrees in sums from £100 to £30,000, and injunctions, which were imposed upon parties unwilling to be bound by the court.[115] The threat of double damages was devised in 1573 to secure compliance.[116] In mercantile cases, commissioners might be appointed to assess the value of goods and to supervise restitution either by specific performance, redelivery of goods, or the payment of adequate compensation.[117]

Some losers elected to lie in prison rather than obey the court's decrees for the possession of real property or chattels real.[118] Yet in such cases a writ of execution might be directed to the sheriff of the county to put a party in possession and to levy costs and damages, if awarded, on the lands and goods of the defeated litigant.[119] If necessary the *posse comitatus* might be raised to assist the sheriff.[120] Star Chamber was also willing, like Chancery, to order sequestration and receivership.[121] In the last resort, parties refusing to obey the court's decrees became liable to process of contempt, after affidavit concerning the breach, and to discretionary imprisonment in the Fleet or Tower.[122]

CHAPTER FOUR
Analysis of Star Chamber Proceedings

Although the surviving Star Chamber archive is incomplete, what remains is vast and complex. General guidance can be given in an attempt to signpost the user's path through the maze of Tudor proceedings. Yet analysis, like the archival inventory, is concerned with enumeration and classification, and depends to a perhaps excessive degree upon the technique of case-counting. While case-counting can usefully provide the statistics from which analysis of the court's jurisdiction, business and litigants may begin, no more than a very rough impression of the overall activity of Star Chamber, and of its shifting preoccupations, can be furnished by that method. For legal cases are not at any one time equivalent units like pounds, dollars or bags of sand. The term 'suit' or 'action' covers a wide range of human activity: it includes short-term or collateral denunciations brought for advantage with respect to cases pending elsewhere, but also embraces genuine litigation upon substantive issues which lasted perhaps a year or longer.[1] Case statistics are fallible and somewhat arbitrary, especially when, as in Star Chamber, most plaintiffs filed several charges at once against their opponents.[2] Some of these charges were abandoned, while others were pursued, but the incomplete state of the present archive makes it often impossible to be sure upon which issues cases came to trial. The Tudor court's willingness to allow litigants to proceed with both civil and criminal process simultaneously was its greatest asset. That asset will, however, remain the historian's bane.

Despite these limitations, the outlines of Star Chamber's activity in the sixteenth century can be discerned from documents at the Public Record Office. The task of reconstruction is assisted by the material on the court's jurisdiction and business available in the Ellesmere Manuscripts at the Huntington Library. The statistics obtained from case-counting at the Public Record Office can be checked against the impressions left by the compilers of the *Libri Intrationum*, who worked from the original Council registers and Star Chamber order and decree books before they were lost.[3]

We have seen that Wolsey was responsible for the development of Star Chamber as a structured and professionally-organized court of law. The keynote of his policy was announced in a speech delivered before Henry VIII and the Council in Star Chamber on 2 May 1516. Wolsey promulgated a two-tiered strategy of law enforcement and impartial administration of justice. His words were echoed by the king. Together their remarks encapsulated the essential philosophy of Star Chamber for the remainder of the century:[4]

> Secundo die Maii . . . The moste reverent father had this daye to the kinges heighnes a notable and Elegant Oration in Englishe wherin he made open to his moste excellent providence the enormityes usuallye exercised in this his Realme to the derogacion of indifferent Justice as well as the causes of the Continuaunce of the same enormityes. For the redresse and reformacion wherof the same moste reverent father advertised his heighnes in the name of the hole Counsellors of certayne provisions by theire diligent studye excogitate, remittinge onlye to his moste provident wisdome the further orderinge and determinacion of the same without whose moste Royall assent and consent they colde not fullye accomplishe theire said ordinate entent. And thereuppon did exhibite to his grace a bill conteyninge aswell the said enormityes as the remedyes &c. Unto the which Oracion by the said most Reverend father had The kinges moste noble grace perfectlye shewinge him selfe not onlye to have in Remembrance his oathe taken at the tyme of his most triumphant coronacion, but alsoe to be of verye perfecte and indifferent zeale to this his Realme and Subiectes, here Answered that his moste desyer and comforte was in the prosperous and continuall advauncement of this his Realme, the restfull tranquilitye of his Subiectes and th'indifferent ministracion of Justice to all persounes aswell heighe as lowe which be to him in semblable Regarde as to that purpose; and for that his noblenes advertised aswell his moste honorable Councellors as his Judges and ministers of his Lawes of his moste heighe pleasure Appertayninge the same to be onlye inclined to dewe ministracion of Justice, willinge his saide Counsellers, Judges and ministers to followe and execute the same. And yf for mayntenaunce, supportacion, imbraserye or other sinister meanes they colde not put his Lawes in dewe execucion, then his Grace wills his said Counsaylers to repayre to his moste noble and mightye power shewinge th'occasions of the lett of ther said Justice, and his grace shall not onlye endevour him selfe to th'advauncement of Justice but alsoe addresse his moste terrible power yf neede sholde, as god forbid, for the subduinge and repressinge of th'enemyes of Justice yf anye suche be founden.

Wolsey reiterated his policy of enforcement three times in Star Chamber during the years of his ascendancy. His enthusiasm for justice, and his popularization of Star Chamber as a forum for litigation, spawned a renaissance of the judicial function of the King's Council.[5]

Under Wolsey's guidance, the nature and content of Star Chamber's legal business came to fall into five areas. The main category consisted of riot, rout, unlawful assembly, forcible entry, assault, trespass and related offences, usually in cases where the possession of real property or chattels was really at stake. A sample of suits filed under Wolsey reveals that in forty-eight per cent of cases, plaintiffs alleged riot, rout or unlawful assembly against their opponents at this date.[6] Yet the same sample yields evidence of genuine rioting in only seven per cent of these cases.[7] In fact, title to property was at base in forty-one per cent of cases. When the 'real' as opposed to the 'alleged' subjects of this sample are expressed in tabular form, the first category of Star Chamber's business under Wolsey appears thus:

Subject	No of cases
Riot, rout, unlawful assembly	35
Forcible entry, dispossession, forcible detainder	4
Assault, battery, false imprisonment	11
Trespass to chattels, detinue, conversion, illegal distress	48
Title	194

Since the sample of cases was chosen solely on the criterion of adequate documentation, it follows that these figures must be used with caution. The underlying pattern is, however, manifestly established.

The second category of business dealt with perversion of justice, abuse of legal procedure, offences prejudicial to public justice, and crimes which remained unpunished at common law, usually for reasons of corruption. Taking our existing sample of cases, we find that this type of work comprised only nine per cent of Star Chamber's total activity under Wolsey. Nevertheless, it was a vital area: for instance, corrupt juries were hauled into the court in 1516, 1517, 1520, 1523, 1527 and 1529.[8] Twenty-three per cent of cases in this category concerned the abuse of legal procedure; fourteen per cent were cases of maintenance or champerty; eleven per cent were instances of corrupt verdicts by juries; another eleven per cent were cases of perjury, subornation or embracery; and twenty-seven per cent of these cases alleged felony unpunished at common law or abetting felony. The remaining cases were contempt proceedings within Star Chamber itself.

The third type of case heard in Star Chamber under Wolsey was precisely defined: thirty-eight bills of complaint charged royal or franchisal officers with corruption or extortion. Twenty-eight of these suits were in reality concerned with official malfeasance (six per cent of the sample). Lack of adequate documentation means that the remaining ten cases cannot be more precisely described.[9]

The fourth category of business encompassed municipal and trade disputes. This jurisdiction was appropriate to the Council, since 'where good ordre lacketh and division be amongst any Comynaltie, there shall ensue desolacion and destruccion of the same Cominaltie'.[10] Our sample includes eight municipal disputes, six trade disputes, and three cases of engrossing, forestalling or regrating of foodstuffs. These cases make up four per cent of the total sample.

Finally, the fifth area of business, although being an essentially miscellaneous collection of cases that defies rigid classification, derives some coherence from the actual or potential violence alleged by most plaintiffs in their bills to attract the court's attention, but in circumstances other than those of the first category of offences. The 'real' subjects at issue in these cases ranged from crimes and torts to unsocial acts and civil disputes.[11] They may conveniently be expressed as a table:

Subject	No of cases
Breach of contract	5
Debt	11
Defamation	3
Easements dispute	10
Enclosure dispute	17
Extortion, embezzlement (except by officers)	3
Forgery	5
Fraud	3
Hunting offence	6
Interruption of family relations	5
Landlord and tenant, rent dispute	10
Nuisance	2
Testamentary dispute	4
Tithes dispute	8

Taken as a whole these ninety-two cases comprise twenty per cent of the sample.

We noted that the Ellesmere Manuscripts record the impressions received by the compilers of the *Libri Intrationum* as they read through the original Council registers and Star Chamber order and decree books in Elizabeth I's reign. One of these compilers in the course of his researches into the Henrician court prepared a list of subjects heard in the reign of Henry VIII. Two copies of this list, which is arranged chronologically, are extant.[12] As a number of entries in the list can be clearly identified and dated, it is possible to extract a table of matters taken during Wolsey's ascendancy. This is done by locating the first and last definite entries for his chancellorship, while omitting the purely executive *acta* of the King's Council, which the compilers of the *Libri* mistook for the business of the court of Star Chamber.[13] The ensuing list of subjects is preferable to any other except that derived from the sample of adequately documented suits filed under Wolsey remaining among the court's records at the Public Record Office:

'Henricus Octavus Rex Angliae'
'What matters and causes were heard in the
Star Chamber in the time of Henry VIII',
1515–1529

Riots, misdemeanours, rescues, forcible entries
Contempts, perjury and procurement thereof

Mayhem
Extortion
Barretry
False accusation
The discretion of men by office found idiots
The taking away the king's widow without his licence
Falsehood in undersheriffs
Extremity shown by judges against persons indicted
The offenders in praemunire
The breach of decrees of this court
Seditious bills
Counsellors and procurers of false accusers
Exhibiters of bills in this court which they cannot prove committed to the Fleet
The assessors of wrongful amercements
The arresting of one, another cause depending between the parties in this court
Disobeying the king's letters for the gift of an office
The taking away of the king's ward
Wrongful vexation
Maintenance of thieves and remissness in punishing them
The taking upon him the administration of goods as executor, and not so proved
False exclamation of men's deaths
Rigorous, forward troublers and vexers of the king's subjects committed to the
    Fleet
For false entries made in court rolls, liberty given to sue at common law
Hurts to private persons
Unlawful assemblies
Opprobrious words against the king's process
Binding to the peace upon oath made of bodily fear
Labouring a jury to give a false verdict
Not doing of duty in jurors
Taking away of corn
Embracery
Subornation

This list does much to confirm the analysis of business attempted from the documents in STAC 2. Yet it has one major deficiency. The compilers of the *Libri* were biased in an important respect. Their concern was to detect the historical antecedents of the jurisdiction exercised by the late-Elizabethan court of Star Chamber, with the result that they failed to investigate or to distinguish the conflicting attitudes of the Henrician and Elizabethan courts to the hearing and determination of unquiet titles. When our compiler reduced his notes for the period from 1550 to 1576 to a brief 'Observation of causes used to be harde and Judged in the Courte of Starr Chamber', he appended the statement:[14]

Titles to landes or goodes	Are not hard in the starre chambre but referred to the commen lawe

Possession   This court doeth not use to medle with any
possession, but leaveth the same to the Lawe.
Except that if the partie be put forth of possession
by a ryot or such unlawfull act, in that case the
court wold reastore hym, as he was before the same
unlawfull act commytted.

This was a correct appraisal of the policy of the Elizabethan court, but it did
not represent the practice of Star Chamber in the reigns of Henry VII and
VIII.

A better opinion was that furnished by the compiler of British Library,
Harleian MS. 2143. With reference to Henry VIII's reign he wrote: 'Note
that in the kinges time this Court dealt with titles, and setled possessions
betweene lordes and Tenantes, and differences in Corporacions and fellow-
shippis weare heare determined'.[15] This conclusion supports the impression
we gained from analysis of the sample of cases for Wolsey's years. The
compiler of Harleian MS. 2143 also remarked:

> The Lordes of the Starr chamber did in Ed[ward] 6 his time and Queene M[ary's]
> time for the most part determine of all titles, and some time retaine the punishment
> of the Ryottes.[16]

His cryptic comment confirms that Star Chamber was still hearing unquiet
titles in Mary's reign. However, it implies, too, that in some cases, the
allegations of riot alone were reserved to the court's judgment, while the
disputed titles were remitted for decision in the common law courts. The
second procedure was that followed by the court in Elizabeth's reign.[17] It
thus seems that in the 1550s Star Chamber's policy was in a state of flux. This
supposition is reinforced by another note in Harleian MS. 2143: 'Tythes
determined as appeareth by these Causes done Commonly upon a Certificat
of the iudges to whom the plaintiffe referred'.[18] One of the cases mentioned,
Ward v. *Ousley* makes plain that in 1552 the bench had adopted the procedure that was associated with the Henrician, not the Elizabethan Star Chamber. The losing party was compelled in open court to seal a deed of con-
veyance in favour of the victor. This was an act quite unlike subsequent
decisions that ordered the cancellation of forged instruments upon which title
might depend. It was, instead, almost exactly comparable to action taken
during Wolsey's chancellorship.

For instance, Wolsey had pronounced a decree on 29 November 1524
which directly altered a real interest in property. In *Blundell* v. *Molyneux*, the
defendants were commanded to 'appere afore the same lorde and Councell in
theire propre persons in the Sterre Chamber at Westminster at the begyn-
nyng of hillarie terme nexte commyng, ther to relesse all there right, title,
intereste and possession that they have or ever hadde in the londes and
tenementes late of Nicholas Blundell squyer by reason of a wrytte of entre in

the post'. In addition, the principal defendant was to 'sease and relynquysse all suche feynyd and untrewe accions and sutes as he or ony of his servauntes or part takers have or hath commensid and takyn ageynst the sayd George [Blundell plaintiff] or ony of his part takers in any wise in ony Court of our Sovereigne lorde the kyng within the Realme of Englond'.[19] In several other cases, Wolsey took considerable care to avoid pronouncements on legal title as such, but sometimes his Star Chamber went beyond orders to the parties concerning possession and occupation of land. On such occasions decrees were pronounced 'by th'advise of the kynges Judges and Justices'.[20] The opinion deliberately encouraged by his enemies after his fall that Wolsey had acted irresponsibly in Star Chamber is fallacious.[21]

Yet the Elizabethan court did not try titles after the opening years of the reign had passed. In *Cholmeley* v. *Holford*, heard in Michaelmas term 1579, the plaintiff was restored to his occupation of land by Star Chamber on the grounds that he had been evicted during a riot.[22] The following year Thomas Throckmorton was returned to possession 'being put forth by a riot of the Lord Barkley's men'.[23] In January 1581 Robert Ryseley was fined 1000 marks and sentenced to imprisonment in the Fleet for fraudulently obtaining lands worth £30 per annum. He was ordered to 'restore the landes or to be close prisoner untyll he reassure yt'.[24] These decisions were, however, the nearest that the Elizabethan Star Chamber came to affecting a real property interest after about 1560. In fact, the shift in jurisdiction had probably begun in October 1551, when a government order was announced in Star Chamber that the English bill courts were no longer to entertain litigation to the prejudice of the common law courts. The order is known only from the Ellesmere Manuscripts. As noted by Lord Ellesmere it reads:[25]

> 30 October 5 E[dward] 6
> The L[ord] Tr[easur]er declared the kinges pleasure, touching the disorders that have bene used in this Court, in the Chauncery, and Whyte halle, in houldinge pleas to the derogacion of the commen lawe. Nota bene the tyme etc.

We can but deplore the lack of historical vision that deprived us of a more spacious transcript of this vital entry in the Star Chamber order book.

In 1558 Star Chamber's business came within five revised areas as compared to the years of Wolsey's chancellorship. The main category embraced crimes of violence: riot, rout, unlawful assembly, assault and wrongful arrest. A sample of suits comprising all those filed in the first year of Elizabeth's reign (17 November 1558 – 16 November 1559) shows that in fifty-two per cent of cases, plaintiffs alleged these offences in their bills of complaint.[26] Perhaps property issues lay behind some, or many, of these suits in Star Chamber. But if so, they were not regarded as primarily property suits by the court. On the contrary, they seem at this date to have been received essentially at face value. Seven suits were filed during the year which did concern title and were so regarded by the court. They amount to nine per cent of Star Chamber's workload in terms of the sample. The contrast with Wolsey's time, when forty-one per cent of cases directly addressed title to property, is nevertheless striking.

The second category of business covered substantive crimes against property: extortion, forgery, fraud, and abduction (really a property offence, because the heir's estate was at stake).[27] Such crimes total twenty-one per cent within our present sample. Fraud was the principal charge in over half these cases. By comparison only nine suits were filed in Elizabeth's first year that alleged crimes against justice, the third type of work in Star Chamber at this date. There were four charges of perjury or subornation, four of procuration, and one of maintenance. Together they constitute eleven per cent of the total sample.

The fourth and fifth categories of Star Chamber business in 1558–9 were crimes against the state and public policy, and official malfeasance. Three cases of contempt of royal proclamations (four per cent of the sample of cases) furnish the only examples of the former type of offence filed in the queen's first year. Two cases of corrupt practices by officials might seem superficially to suggest that there were fewer charges of malfeasance in the early-Elizabethan court than under Wolsey. However, our evidence within this category is too meagre for so precise a conclusion to be thought reliable.

The incipient transformation of Star Chamber into an almost exclusively criminal court in the second half of the sixteenth century is apparent from this analysis of proceedings. And once again confirmation can be obtained from a contemporary list of subjects among the Ellesmere Manuscripts. The same compiler who prepared the list of matters heard in Henry VIII's reign wrote out another tabulation of subjects judged in the first two decades of Elizabeth's reign:[28]

'Observation of causes used to be harde and
Judged in the Courte of Starr Chamber',
c. 1550–1576

Riots, routs, forcible entries, unlawful assemblies
Forgeries (lands, goods)
Perjury of juries and particular persons, procurers
Battery called the bastonado
Deceits called cozenage
Misdemeanours of sheriffs
Misdemeanours of justices of the peace
Embracery of juries
Maintenance
Champerty
Slanderous libel
Misdemeanours of commissioners
Deceit in levying of fines

Misdemeanours against justices of assize, of the peace, and other officers
Extortion
Unlawful hunting in parks and forests
Confederacies of tenants against their lords
Crafty, subtle and dishonest invention and policy punished
Getting of money by false tokens and counterfeit letters
Disorders in printing and uttering of books
Slandering and lewd speaking of noble persons and councillors
False presentments
Disobeying of process
False returns of sheriffs
Razing of writs and counterfeiting of hands
Wearing apparel contrary to proclamation
Practices to defeat decrees in other courts by fraudulent shrifts
Taking of young women from parents or those to whose custody they are committed
Sorcery, conjuration, and procurement thereof
Massmongers, or hearers of mass
Selling wines by retail contrary to the statute of 7 Edward VI[29]
Misbehaviours of tenants in the courts of their lords
Conspiracy of murder
Corruption and bribery
Deflowering of ladies
Breaking of prison
Receiving, buying, reading, keeping, recommending, and sending abroad seditious books
Not receiving the communion
Embezzling records out of the Tower

The process by which Star Chamber's jurisdiction became exclusively criminal was complete by the end of Elizabeth's reign.[30] Our third sample of cases comprises those filed in the last full regnal year of her rule (17 November 1601 – 16 November 1602).[31] This shows that Star Chamber's business by 1601 fell fairly neatly within six broad areas: the five discerned already in 1558, plus a small number of cases of defamation. Nevertheless, these 'new' cases of defamation were, in fact, but a continuation of the jurisdiction pioneered under Wolsey, when three such cases were heard in Star Chamber.[32] The absence of defamation suits from the sample of cases brought in 1558–9 is almost certainly accidental. We can conclude no more than that none was filed in that regnal year.

The largest category of offences at the beginning of the seventeenth century remained crimes of violence. Riot, rout, unlawful assembly, assault, wrongful arrest, resistance, oppression and challenge prior to duelling amount to forty per cent of the crimes charged in 1601–2. There were 112 cases of riot/unlawful assembly, 94 cases of forcible entry, and 74 cases of assault or wrongful arrest. There were 29 cases of resistance, but oppression and duelling are represented by only one case each. Doubtless these allegations of 'crime' cloaked the essentially civil ends of the litigants who filed them: Lord Keeper Williams confirmed in 1625 that 'riot' in Star Chamber proceedings had become essentially a term of art.[33] But it is certain that litigants no longer directly addressed the issue of title to property. Only one per cent of suits filed in Elizabeth's last full year raised the matter directly; even then the nine plaintiffs in question seem to have done so on the basis of some ensuing affray.[34] Indeed it was a matter for special pleading whether 'title' lay within the court's purview. Richard Harvey, a defendant, refused to acknowledge certain questions for that they were 'matter of title not examinable in this Court'. The interesting point is that he was compelled to make another and better answer.[35]

Substantive crimes against property were defined in 1601–2 as extortion, forgery, fraud, abduction, and cozenage or cony-catching (the last, like abduction, a property offence insofar as the victim's assets were threatened).[36] There were in this year 22 cases of extortion, 73 cases of forgery, and 40 cases of fraud. Abduction accounted for 4 cases, and cozenage or cony-catching for 21 cases. These crimes total twenty per cent of the offences found within the whole sample.

The third category of business covered crimes against justice. Over the twelve months from November 1601 to November 1602 there were 121 cases of perjury or subornation by individuals or jurors; there were 35 cases each of maintenance and procuration; and there were 16 cases of conspiracy and 2 of giving liveries with intent to pervert the course of justice. These 209 cases together constitute twenty-seven per cent of the total sample.

Next, two cases alleged contempt of royal proclamations.[37] Seventy-four cases concerned official malfeasance or corrupt practices (nine per cent of the total sample). Defamation suits, by contrast, were disproportionately few in relation to their contribution to English legal development. Eighteen suits were filed in Elizabeth's last full regnal year, which amount to two per cent of the sample.[38]

If our samples of Star Chamber cases are structured to illustrate the geographical origins of the litigation brought to the court, we find that suitors arrived from all parts of England and Wales, and from Ireland and Jersey, too, under Henry VIII. Large numbers of sixteenth-century cases arose in South-West England or the Midland counties. East Anglia and the southern counties provided many suits, though Middlesex with London perhaps furnished fewer than might have been expected. Northern England and Wales accounted for relatively few cases, no doubt because litigants from those regions took their suits to the two provincial Councils.[39] However, these patterns of litigation also reflected the population density and economic activity of the various parts of Tudor England and Wales.

The analysis of the geographical distribution of cases is best given as a table. The percentage of cases filed from a particular region under Wolsey has been compared to that from the same area in the last full regnal year of Elizabeth I.

Geographical distribution of suits

Region	Cases from region expressed as percentage of total sample of Wolsey cases[40]	Cases from region expressed as percentage of total sample of cases filed from Nov. 1601 – Nov. 1602[41]
South-West England[42]	21	18
West Midlands[43]	16	15
East Anglia[44]	16	11
East Midlands[45]	12	16
Northern England[46]	11	11
Southern England[47]	9	10
Middlesex with London	5	8
Wales[48]	4	9
Ireland[49]	0.5	—
Jersey[49]	0.5	—
No county specified	5	2

Looking at the pattern of cases arising from individual counties is more complex, in view of the small number of suits involved in certain instances and the differing size of counties. Since over forty counties are embodied in the table, it follows that if three per cent or more of cases from the samples belong to a particular county, then this represents a significant slice of Star Chamber's litigation in terms of other counties. A common figure of less than one per cent of cases marks, conversely, that county's under-representation in relation to other areas. On this basis counties responsible for a significant contribution to Star Chamber litigation under Wolsey and in 1601–2 were Norfolk, Devon, Gloucestershire, Lincolnshire, Yorkshire, and Middlesex with London. Close behind were Cornwall, Somerset and Derbyshire. By contrast areas providing little business for the court were Northumberland, Durham, Westmorland, Huntingdonshire, Rutland, and many of the Welsh counties. This analysis is clearly affected by the population density, size or remoteness of particular places, and by any availability of alternative facilities for litigation locally.

Case-analysis can also elucidate the social status of litigants in Star Chamber. Comparison of all plaintiffs and known relators who filed suits under Wolsey and in the reign of James I (1603–25) indicates that the principals to litigation in the court were normally of high social position.[50] The figures for Wolsey's years are somewhat limited in value, owing to the large percentage of cases in which the plaintiff's status is untraceable. Within its own terms, however, the analysis for Wolsey's time shows that gentlemen and clergy were then prominent in Star Chamber. There were more clergy to be found as litigants in the court before the Reformation than afterwards. Few nobles, by contrast, litigated in Star Chamber as plaintiffs under Wolsey. It seems that by the early seventeenth century the proportion of nobility and gentry among plaintiffs had risen in relation to other social groups, but this conclusion must remain impressionistic in view of the defective documentation for Henry VIII's reign.

Social status of plaintiffs

Status	Percentage of total plaintiffs in sample of Wolsey cases	Percentage of total plaintiffs under James I
Gentleman and above	16	54
Professional and clergy	14	4
Merchants	6	6
Yeomen, husbandmen, craftsman labourers	18	20
Others	2	1
Paupers	0.1	—
Unknown	43.9	15

The fact that Star Chamber plaintiffs tended to come from the upper echelons of society must partly have reflected the costs of litigation in the court. Even under Wolsey Star Chamber was expensive. Only two plaintiffs were allowed to sue *in forma pauperis* during his chancellorship, despite his emphasis on giving justice to the poor.[51] No doubt pauper plaintiffs were expected to take their suits to the dean of the Chapel, and later to the court of Requests.[52]

Not least among the expenses of litigation were the termly fees required to retain counsel and an attorney. Thus in Henry VII's reign, when Star Chamber suits were dealt with expeditiously, Sir John Damsell had been obliged to retain counsel at 3s. 4d. per term for fourteen terms, and pay the fee of his attorney at 20d. per term for the same period.[53] The cost of written pleadings, writs, commissions, examinations, orders and decrees, and any copies needed, depended on a combination of basic charges and supplementary ones according to the length of the instruments in question. Most documents turned out to be longer than could be obtained for the minimum fees. Additional were the costs, where necessary, of hiring process-servers.

The tables compare basic costs incurred in Star Chamber in Henry VIII's and Elizabeth's reigns. The dates chosen represent, first, the end of Wolsey's chancellorship, and secondly the period shortly before Lord Keeper Egerton's comprehensive reform of fees on 3 May 1598. The second table of fees is dated 3 December 1597, which followed an initial attempt at reform undertaken by Egerton the previous May.[54]

Costs in Star Chamber c. 1530[55]

Item	s.	d.
For *subpoena ad comparendum*	2	6
For *subpoena ad testificandum*	2	6
For *subpoena ad audiendum iudicium*	2	6
For privy seal	7	0
For writ of attachment	2	6
For an injunction	5	0
For a writ of *dedimus* potestatem	3	4
For entry of appearance of every person	2	0
For an affidavit	1	8
For admission to attorney	2	0
For copy of opponent's bill/ answer	1	0 (minimum)
For examination of every witness	2	0
For entry and warrant for a commission	2	6
Drawing of every recognisance	6	8
Copy of same	2	0
For the decree	4	0 (minimum)
Recording the decree in register	1	4 (minimum)

Costs in Star Chamber in 1597[56]

Item	s.	d.
For making a warrant for all types of process by writ of *subpoena*	2	0
For all types of *subpoena*	2	6
For writ of attachment	2	6
For an injunction	13	4
For a writ of *dedimus potestatem*	7	2
For a *supersedeas*	7	2
For a commission of rebellion	13	0
For entry of appearance of every person	2	0
For an affidavit	2	4
For every defendant who appears by affidavit	2	4
For entry and warrant of every attachment without affidavit	3	4

Item	s.	d.
For copy of every affidavit	2	0
For entry and warrant of every attachment upon affidavit	2	4
For entry and warrant for all attachments with proclamation	3	4
For entry and warrant of every *alias* process of contempt	2	0
For entry and warrant of all commissions of rebellion, *certiorari*, writ of privilege, or injunction	3	4
For recording an obligation	2	0
For entry and warrant of every *supersedeas*	3	4
For holding of the oath book and carrying the defendant's answer to the attorney	1	0
For entry of every *dedimus potestatem* and every commission upon the return	1	0
For examination of every defendant	2	4
For defendant's licence to depart	2	4
For all manner of copies, written by the sheet, for every sheet	1	0
For every admission to attorney	2	4
For every recognisance	4	0
For cancelling every recognisance	3	4
For examination of every witness	2	4
For recording the oath of each witness		4
For entry and warrant for a commission	3	10
For drawing and entering a rule of court	1	0
For entry and warrant for renewing a commission	2	0
For copy of every certificate of commitment, or from the commissioners	2	0
For copy of every order and rule of court	2	0
For making indentures for bringing in of deeds	3	4
For search of all records or pleadings in the bundles or registers	2	0
For the clerk's signature upon all manner of copy pleadings or examinations	2	0

Item	s.	d.
The clerk's fee for taking any person's oath out of court, or out of his office	10	0
For entry of publication and day of hearing	1	0
For every defendant who answers by *dedimus potestatem* without affidavit	2	0
For certificate made into Chancery	10	0
For certified copies on parchment, per leaf	5	0
For every person dismissed	2	0
Poundage for costs and damages, per pound	1	0

The proliferation of Star Chamber's bureaucracy under Elizabeth is fully apparent from this second table of fees. Basic costs of litigation in the court had soared between 1530 and 1597. Some allowance should be made for Tudor inflation. Prices generally had more than doubled in the six decades after Wolsey's fall, but this was no excuse for the shameless multiplication of clerical tasks and fees. In the last resort, the contrast between Star Chamber's efficiency and agility under Wolsey and its dilatoriness and the abuses that saturated the court during Elizabeth's last years cannot be overstated.

Even so the problems afflicting Star Chamber at James I's accession only escalated after 1608. The intrusion of sinecurists into the court's bureaucracy when the reversion of the clerkship accrued to Sir Francis Bacon eliminated any prospect of lasting reform. By the time the Long Parliament abolished Star Chamber in 1641, the court in a very real sense had outlived its natural life.

APPENDIX A

Misplaced documents in STAC 2, listed in *List of Proceedings in the Court of Star Chamber*, vol. 1, 1485–1558, P.R.O. Lists and Indexes, no. 13 (New York, Kraus Reprint, 1963), as belonging to Henry VIII's reign.

The following belong to the reign of Edward IV:

    STAC 2/1/150–52
          17/154
          20/305
          26/393

The following belongs to the reign of Richard III:

    STAC 2/22/176

The following belong to the reign of Henry VII:

    STAC 2/1/179
          2/45
          2/46–47
          2/233
          2/278
          3/170 & 172a
          3/180
          3/182–83
          3/210–18B
          3/303–09
          4/182
          5/4–6
          5/23–26
          5/67–68
          5/128
          5/147
          5/159
          5/166
          6/247
          7/177
          8/159
          8/247–50
          10/51

STAC 2/10/136–36A
       10/163–66
       10/270–71
       10/340
       12/85–86
       12/216
       13/77
       14/35
       14/111–12
       14/113–15
       14/169–71
       14/193
       15/15
       15/36
       15/77–80
       15/128
       15/369
       16/36
       16/86
       16/87–88
       17/8
       17/10
       17/85
       17/91
       17/140
       17/149
       17/151
       17/155
       17/180
       17/182
       17/190
       17/202
       17/210
       17/238
       17/242
       17/258
       17/268, 291
       17/276
       17/284
       17/295
       17/310
       17/331*
       17/335

*transferred from Requests

STAC 2/17/338	STAC 2/19/131
17/341	19/141
17/358	19/142
17/360	19/149
17/367	19/154
17/369	19/237
17/372	19/266
17/409	19/276
18/27	19/284
18/37	19/354
18/41	19/361
18/48	19/362
18/54	19/365
18/121	19/369
18/135	19/372
18/138	19/377
18/157	20/9
18/159	20/12
18/171	20/17
18/176	20/21
18/207	20/22
18/215	20/29
18/217	20/36
18/244	20/38
18/253	20/54
18/268	20/111, 87
18/269	20/113
18/273	20/114
18/285	20/129
18/288	20/154
18/289	20/177
18/322	20/257
18/323	20/265
18/327	20/267
19/26	20/269
19/29	20/292
19/38	20/301
19/42	20/315
19/63	20/377
19/66	20/381
19/70	20/383
19/71	21/9
19/72	21/76, 77
19/73	21/156
19/82	21/172
19/86	22/13
19/105	22/90
19/110	22/127
19/113	22/134
19/116	22/173
19/125	22/228

STAC 2/22/286	STAC 2/26/40
22/301	26/70
23/4	26/81
23/69	26/83
23/103	26/109
23/141	26/130
23/180	26/145
23/223	26/154
23/263	26/161
24/19	26/196
24/32	26/197, 195
24/56	26/216
24/57	26/226
24/62	26/229
24/65	26/232
24/106	26/233
24/121	26/298
24/134	26/321
24/151	26/343
24/176	26/346, 342
24/195	26/352
24/295	26/371
24/305	26/406
24/309, 314	26/469
24/336	27/18
24/367	27/19
24/405	27/53
24/419	27/76
25/2	27/84
25/31	27/101
25/54	27/137
25/57	29/22
25/68	29/28
25/81	29/124
25/84	29/188
25/180	29/bundle of papers and
25/199	fragments (unlisted)
25/206	30/41
25/207	31/2
25/210	32/34
25/237	32/106
25/255	32/bundle of papers and
25/270	fragments (unlisted)
25/277	33/24
25/296	33/30
25/330	33/46
26/1	33/60
26/2	33/63
26/11	34/58
26/32	34/65
26/35	34/78

STAC 2/34/117
34/131
34/142
34/149
34/152
34/162
34/163
35/40

The following belong to the reign of
Edward VI:
STAC 2/1/161
1/164–74
2/117a–18
2/197–203
5/89
5/170
7/124
7/229
8/122
8/124
8/290–92
9/102–06
10/144–44B
11/49
13/222
14/167–68
15/210–12
15/232–33
16/23–25
16/171
16/411–13B
17/124
17/128
17/143
17/277
17/329
18/81
18/85, 105
18/148
18/158
19/62
19/109
19/171
19/175
19/186
20/94
20/171
20/216

STAC 2/20/359
20/390
22/19
22/202
22/224, 218
22/305
23/55, 50
23/111
24/5
24/23
24/43
24/104
26/85
26/120
26/169
28/11
32/54
35/bundle of papers and
fragments (unlisted)

The following belong to the reign of
Philip & Mary:
STAC 2/13/85
25/223
35/bundle of papers and
fragments (unlisted)

The following belong to the reign of
Elizabeth I:
STAC 2/17/11
17/38
17/289
18/243
20/178
20/241
20/380
22/110
22/253
24/328
24/358
25/38
25/227
26/123
26/440
34/177

The following belongs to the reign of
James I:
STAC 2/34/109

APPENDIX B

Misplaced documents in STAC 2, listed in *List of Proceedings in the Court of Star Chamber*, vol. 1, 1485–1558, P.R.O. Lists and Indexes, no. 13 (New York, Kraus Reprint, 1963), as belonging to Henry VIII's reign. The following properly belong to the Proceedings of the Court of Requests (not all are Henry VIII). Those marked with an asterisk were sent to Requests, having first been filed in Star Chamber. It was not uncommon under Cardinal Wolsey (1515–1529) for plaintiffs in Star Chamber to be remitted to another conciliar court. See J. A. Guy, *The Cardinal's Court* (Hassocks, 1977), pp. 40–50.

STAC 2/8/108
12/162
13/302–03
16/1
17/3
17/6
17/9
*17/27
*17/28
17/32
17/44
17/48
17/49
*17/96
17/131
17/288
17/302
17/313
17/315
*17/320
17/327
17/381
18/62
18/81
18/109

STAC 2/18/144
19/170
*19/194
20/83
20/84
20/254
21/258
22/20
22/152
22/153
22/155
22/156
22/158
24/169
24/349
24/385
24/402
24/419
24/425
25/2
25/127
25/259
25/280
25/281
*25/292
25/307
26/97
26/221
26/397
27/4
27/11
27/20
27/21
27/23
27/24
27/25
27/26
27/28
27/34
27/43
27/44
27/52
27/54

STAC 2/27/57	STAC 2/33/32
27/58	33/35
27/60	33/46
27/61	33/48
27/69	33/57
27/71	33/58
27/133	33/60
27/162	34/57
28/135	34/62
30/100	34/84
30/148	34/121
31/28	34/171
31/31	35/24
31/46	35/28
31/77	35/29
31/84	35/34
31/105	35/36
33/25	35/37
33/26	35/45
33/27	35/55
★33/28	35/68
33/29	

APPENDIX C

Misplaced documents in STAC 2, listed
in *List of Proceedings in the Court of Star
Chamber,* Lists and Indexes, no. 13, vol.
1, 1485–1558 (New York, Kraus
Reprint, 1963), as belonging to Henry
VIII's reign. The following properly
belong to the Proceedings of the Court of
Chancery:

   STAC 2/3/241–43
          3/286–87 & 143–48
          4/124
          12/121–21B
          16/197
          19/204
          21/237
          22/168
          24/313 & 315

APPENDIX D

The following documents in STAC 10 (Star Chamber, Miscellanea) have been identified. Documents in this class remain unlisted, but are produced in the search rooms upon calling for individual bundles under the codes STAC 10/1 et seq. Part numbers and individual piece or other sub-numbers as cited in this appendix do not refer to any published or unpublished list, but are numbers previously assigned to individual pieces or folios by the Conservation Department at the Office, when the documents were recently repaired. Such numbers, however, provide a convenient means of reference for the purposes of this appendix. The editor is grateful to Professor Thomas G. Barnes for his assistance in compiling the notes on which this appendix is based.

The following are Star Chamber documents belonging to the reign of Henry VII:

STAC 10/1/4
1/19
1/78
1/98
4/part 1, passim
4/part 2, passim
4/part 5/4
4/part 5/13
4/part 5/18
4/part 5/44
4/part 5/57
4/part 5/61
4/part 5/63
4/part 5/71
4/part 6, passim
4/part 7, passim
4/part 8/38
4/part 10, passim
6/172–74
8/195–395

STAC 10/8/977–996
19/passim

The following are Star Chamber documents belonging to the reign of Henry VIII.

STAC 10/1/3
1/5
1/6
1/8
1/9
1/11
1/12
1/15
1/18
1/20
1/21
1/26
1/33
1/39
1/56
1/63
1/66
1/71
1/77
1/99
1/167
3/123
3/124
3/125
3/126
3/127
3/128
3/129
3/130
3/131
3/132
3/133
3/134
3/135
3/136
4/part 1/passim
4/part 2/72–3

STAC 10/ 4/part 2/74–5
4/part 2/82–4
4/part 2/127–32
4/part 2/170–73
4/part 2/218–21
4/part 4/1
4/part 5/9–10
4/part 5/21
4/part 5, passim
4/part 7/66
4/part 10, passim
4/part 10/35
4/part 10/38–39
4/part 10/62
6/172–74
8/977–996
10/passim
18/130–35
18/137–41
19/passim

The following are Star Chamber
documents belonging to the reign of
Edward VI:
STAC 10/5/3
15/48–57
16/100–21
16/225–28
16/229–30
16/231–36
16/237–38

The following are Star Chamber
documents belonging to the reign of
Philip & Mary:
STAC 10/15/18–33
15/34–39
15/58–61
15/108–13
15/131–32
18/225
20/part 2, passim

The following are Star Chamber
documents belonging to the reign of
Elizabeth I:
STAC 10/2/bundle
5/61–62
5/90–92
5/93–119
5/129

STAC 10/5/182–83
5/184
5/185–86
6/2–5
6/36
6/60–61
6/101
6/125–37
6/182
6/183–226
6/236–37
6/283–84
8/847
8/911–30
12/173
12/181–84
12/189
12/213
12/233
12/265–66
12/276–77
13/12
13/17
13/54–57
13/101–03
13/177
13/327
14/147–48
17/passim
18/1
18/2–3
18/4
18/6–30
18/40–41
18/42–43
18/46
18/47
18/48–49
18/74–80
18/81–93
18/124–25
18/226–65
18/776–85
20/part 1, passim
20/part 2, passim

The following properly belong to the
Proceedings of the Court of Requests
(up to 1603):
STAC 10/1/early cases
3/29

STAC 10/3/30
      3/32
      3/37
      3/40
      3/44
      3/59
      3/60
      3/63
      3/87
      3/89
      3/97
      3/99
      3/100
      3/105
      3/112
      3/114
      3/115
      4/part 7/98 (perhaps
        Chancery)
      4/part 7/99–100 (perhaps
        Chancery)
      4/part 7/101 (perhaps
        Chancery)
      7/part 1/713
      8/655 (perhaps Chancery)
      8/716
      8/758
      8/854
      8/876
      8/904
      12/142
      19/1

The following properly belong to the
   Proceedings of the Court of Chancery
   (up to 1603):
   STAC 10/4/part 4/15
        7/part 2/789
        8/655 (perhaps Requests)
        12/233

APPENDIX E

STAC 10/21 at the Public Record Office is a manuscript of William Hudson's 'A Treatise of the Court of Star Chamber'. Although this work was completed by the end of 1621,[1] it was not printed until 1792.[2] It then appeared at the beginning of volume two of Francis Hargrave's *Collectanea Juridica*.

Hudson's career and the politico-legal climate in which his 'Treatise' was composed have been discussed by Professor Thomas G. Barnes.[3] Despite the preoccupations which pervade Hudson's account, it remains an essential guide to the court, its jurisdiction and procedure. For example, the author cites over five hundred cases in Star Chamber, many of which can no longer be traced in any other source. But Hudson's text must be treated critically and as a whole: it can be misleading to use it piecemeal to elucidate particular cases or aspects of Star Chamber's jurisdiction. Seventeenth-century reporters too often had axes to grind.[4]

Thirty manuscripts of Hudson's 'Treatise' are located in various libraries outside the Public Record Office:[5]
Harvard Law School MSS. HLS 82, 133;[6] L 1116, 4007
Cambridge University Library MSS. Ll. 3. 3; Ll. 4. 10; Additional 3106
Bodleian Library MS. Douce 66
All Souls College, Oxford MSS. 178a,[7] 178b,[8] 256[9]
British Library MSS. Lansdowne 254, 622, 905; Harleian 736, 859, 1226, 1689, 4274, 6235, 6256; Hargrave 250, 251, 290, 291; Stowe 419; Additional 4520, 11681, 26647

Henry E. Huntington Library MS. Ellesmere 7921
Two other manuscripts at the British Library seem to contain an early version of the 'Treatise': Harleian MSS.1200, fos. 91–187; 7161, fos. 152–311. B.L. Harleian 1200 lacks Part III of the work, and places Part I, sections 1–4 at the end.[10]

In the absence of the author's original, it is thought that the most reliable complete text is B.L. Harleian MS. 1226. This is the whole 'Treatise', including the last six considerations, which are often omitted. However, the twenty-fourth consideration, upon the execution of sentence, has been numbered as the twenty-fifth, and the error continues to the end of the manuscript, giving the impression that an extra section has been added. B.L. Harleian MS. 1226 includes this memorandum by Sir John Finch:

> This Treatise was compiled by William Hudson of Grais Inne Esq[r] one very much practized and of great experience in the Starrchamber: and my very affectionate friend. His sonne and heyr M[r] Christopher Hudson (whose handwryting this booke is) after his fathers death gave it to mee. 19° Decembris. 1635. Jo: Finch.[11]

It is a pity that Hargrave's printed version of the 'Treatise' was not derived from B.L. Harleian MS. 1226. It was, instead, based on two other manuscripts, both of which are defective. The following table lists the worst errors in the printed text.

Principal inaccuracies in Hargrave's text as printed
in Collectanea Juridica, ii[12]

p. 12 Studley	*should read*	Audley
p. 15 Tristram		Thurstane
p. 19 Erastites		Traskites[13]
p. 19 tropic		topic
p. 36 whispering		whipping
p. 39 Bladeswell		Baldeswell
pp. 38, 42 Ryder		Rydon
p. 39 March		Marshe
p. 50 all capital		as capital
p. 55 who hath at all looked into the ancient records of this court, who will deny that it examined, discussed and determined titles as well as crimes		who hath at all looked into the ancient records of this court but doth well know that it is more common in the time of H.7. and the beginning of the reign of H.8. that this court examined, discussed and determined more titles than crimes
p. 57 tyranny and malice		crime and malice
p. 60 Lentall		Kendall
pp. 60, 65 Boucher		Bourchier
p. 117 Brisacres		Gresacre
p. 137 doth prosecute without charge, as the king's attorney doth		doth not sue without charge, as the king's attorney doth

Footnotes to Appendix E

1 The 'Treatise' was presented to Bishop John Williams on his appointment as lord keeper. See the copyists' notes in B.L. Lansdowne MS. 639, fo. 99[v]; H.E.H. Ellesmere MS. 7921; Guy, *The Cardinal's Court*, 143–4. The last precedent copied from the Star Chamber order and decree books in the course of Hudson's research in preparation for writing the 'Treatise' as recorded in B.L. Lansdowne MS. 639 is dated 1618. This suggests that Hudson wrote up his work between then and 1621. But the version of his text that has come down to us dates from the early years of Charles I's reign (see *Collectanea Juridica*, ii. 103, 166–7, 205). It seems that Hudson then expanded and polished the text of 1621.

2 Francis Hargrave (*ed.*), *Collectanea Juridica* (London, 1791–2), ii. 1–239.
3 Barnes, 'Mr. Hudson's Star Chamber', 285–308. See also Guy, *The Cardinal's Court*, 4–6, 143–4.
4 Barnes, 'Mr Hudson's Star Chamber', 286.
5 Not all these MSS. are complete.
6 Harvard MS. HLS 75 is also listed in the catalogue as a copy of Hudson's 'Treatise', but I have not consulted it. I have seen all other MSS. cited here.
7 Fos. 118–212.
8 Fos. 153–355.
9 Fos. 435–end.
10 The provenance of this possible early version requires further research.
11 Fo. 2[v]. However, the same note appears, too, in B.L. Additional MS. 11681. Guy, *The Cardinal's Court*, 143.

12 Pp. 1–239.
13 This refers to John Trask's case
    heard in 16 James I. 'One John Trask
    a pretended Minister, was Censured
    in the Star Chamber, for depraving
    the Ecclesiastical Government, and
    for holding divers Judaical
    Opinions'. He was pilloried,
    whipped, and ordered to be fed pork.
    R. Baker, *A Chronicle of the Kings of
    England* (London, 1670), 443.

FOOTNOTES

Chapter 1 Star Chamber's Structure

1 G. R. Elton, *The Tudor Constitution* (Cambridge, 2nd ed. 1982), 163–87. The following works are also essential: Elton, 'Henry VII's Council' and 'Why the History of the Early Tudor Council remains unwritten', and 'Tudor Government: the points of contact, the Council', in his *Studies in Tudor and Stuart Politics and Government* (3 vols., Cambridge, 1974, 1983), i. 294–9, 308–38, iii. 21–38; Elton, *The Tudor Revolution in Government* (Cambridge, 1953); J. A. Guy, *The Cardinal's Court* (Hassocks, 1977); A. F. Pollard, 'Council, Star Chamber, and Privy Council under the Tudors', *English Historical Review*, xxxvii (1922), 337–60, 516–39, xxxviii (1923), 42–60; C. G. Bayne and W. H. Dunham (*eds.*), *Select Cases in the Council of Henry VII* (London, Selden Society, 1958); L. M. Hill (*ed.*), *The Ancient State, Authoritie, and Proceedings of the Court of Requests by Sir Julius Caesar* (Cambridge, 1975); D. E. Hoak, *The King's Council in the Reign of Edward VI* (Cambridge, 1976); E. Skelton, 'The Court of Star Chamber in the Reign of Queen Elizabeth' (London M.A. thesis, unpublished. 2 parts, 1931); T. G. Barnes, 'Due Process and Slow Process in the late Elizabethan-early Stuart Star Chamber', *American Journal of Legal History*, vi (1962), 221–49, 315–46; Barnes, 'Star Chamber Litigants and their Counsel, 1596–1641', in *Legal Records and the*

Historian, ed. J. H. Baker (London, 1978), 7–28. Other relevant works are listed in the bibliography. Documents cited in this guide are located at the Public Record Office, London, unless otherwise stated.

2 J. F. Baldwin, *The King's Council in England during the Middle Ages* (Oxford, 1913), 354–58; E. W. Brayley and J. Britton, *History of the Ancient Palace and the Late House of Parliament at Westminster* (London, 1836).

3 Guy, *The Cardinal's Court*, 30–50, 72–8; A. F. Pollard, *Wolsey* (London, 1929), 59–98.

4 This paragraph follows *The History of the King's Works*, vol. iv, Part II (London, 1982), 296–300; T. G. Barnes, 'The Archives and Archival Problems of the Elizabethan and Early Stuart Star Chamber', *Journal of the Society of Archivists*, ii (1963), 358.

5 The absence of the carpet was noted in the court's accounts for Hilary term 1563, when Star Chamber moved temporarily to Hertford to avoid the plague. Four yards of canvas were purchased 'for want of a carpet'. MS. accounts sold at Sotheby's sale of 15 June 1971, lot 1672.

6 The red carpet is illustrated in the painting of the Somerset House Conference (artist unknown) at the National Portrait Gallery, London.

7 Bayne and Dunham, *Select Cases in the Council of Henry VII*, lxiv–lxxii.

8 *STC* 9328. See Skelton, 'The Court of Star Chamber in the Reign of Queen Elizabeth', Part 1, p. 103.

9 Bayne and Dunham, *Select Cases in*

the *Council of Henry VII*, lxviii–lxx.

10 Guy, *The Cardinal's Court*, 6–21.
11 *Ibid.*
12 Bayne and Dunham, *Select Cases in the Council of Henry VII*, xxix.
13 I . M. Hill (*ed.*), *Ancient State*, 39–40.
14 Bayne and Dunham, *Select Cases in the Council of Henry VII*, xxiv–v, xlvii–viii, 25–47.
15 Guy, *The Cardinal's Court*, 23–4.
16 H.E.H. Ellesmere MS. 2655, fos. 7–9^v.
17 Guy, *The Cardinal's Court*, 26–35.
18 *Ibid.*, 15, 51.
19 *Ibid.*, 119–39.
20 *Ibid.*, 27. I have here updated my figures in line with my latest research.
21 *Ibid.*, 36–8, 79–94.
22 B.L. Lansdowne MS. 1, fo. 108.
23 *Ibid.*, fo. 108^v.
24 Guy, *The Cardinal's Court*, 42–3.
25 REQ 1/104, fos. 68^v, 88^v; Guy, *The Cardinal's Court*, 43.
26 Guy, 'The Privy Council: Revolution or Evolution?', in *Revolution Reassessed*, ed. D. R. Starkey and C. Coleman (Oxford, forthcoming).
27 Guy, *The Public Career of Sir Thomas More* (Brighton, 1980), 37–112.
28 Elton, *The Tudor Revolution in Government*, 60–5, 316–69; Guy, 'The Privy Council: Revolution or Evolution?'
29 PC 2/1, p. 1.
30 Guy, 'Wolsey's Star Chamber: a Study in Archival Reconstruction', *Journal of the Society of Archivists*, v (1975), 169–80.
31 The French system is conveniently described in a contemporary treatise, *The Monarchy of France* by Claude de Seyssel, trans. J. H. Hexter, and *ed.* D. R. Kelley (New Haven, 1981).
32 Elton, *The Tudor Constitution*, 164–65.
33 *Ibid.*

34 See lists of attendances in Corpus Christi College, Oxford, MS. 196, pp. 116–56; Bodleian Library, Oxford, MS. Eng. hist. c. 304, fos. 317–46^v; B.L. Additional MS. 4521, fos. 120–51^v; Guildhall Library, London, MS. 1751, pp. 199–250. Two extracts are printed (with minor slips in references to MSS.) in J. H. Baker (*ed.*), *The Reports of Sir John Spelman* (London, Selden Society. 2 vols, 1977–78), ii. 351–52.
35 H.E.H. Ellesmere MS. 2768 (folios numbered in pencil 15, 16, but not so placed in the present binding); Skelton, 'The Court of Star Chamber in the Reign of Queen Elizabeth', Part 1, pp. 20–8.
36 Elton, *The Tudor Constitution*, 165.
37 *De Republica Anglorum* (*STC* 22857), cited from Scolar Press reprint (London, 1970), 94.
38 B.L. Hargrave MS. 216, fo. 103^v.
39 PC 2/1, p. 1.
40 Hoak, *The King's Council in the Reign of Edward VI*, 34–90.
41 H.E.H. Ellesmere MS. 2653.
42 G. A. Lemasters, 'The Privy Council in the Reign of Queen Mary I' (Cambridge Ph.D. thesis, unpublished. 1971), appendix 2.
43 *APC*, v. 88–215.
44 Lemasters, 'The Privy Council in the Reign of Queen Mary I', appendix 2.
45 *APC*, v. 88–215.
46 B.L. Lansdowne MS. 639, fos. 51^v, 52^v,59^v; H.E.H. Ellesmere MS. 2653; H.E.H. Ellesmere MS. 2768 (folio numbered in pencil 43, but not so placed in the present binding).
47 P. Williams, *The Tudor Regime* (Oxford, 1979), 425–28, 453–56.
48 H.E.H. Ellesmere MS. 2768 (folios numbered in pencil 15, 16, but not so placed in the present binding); Skelton, 'The Court of Star Chamber in the Reign of Queen Elizabeth', Part 1, pp. 20–8. The

attendance in Star Chamber on 29 November 1558 is excluded from the calculations, the occasion being political in character.

49 H.E.H. Ellesmere MS. 2653.

50 I arrived at this figure by deducting from the total for the reign the number of cases estimated to have been filed before Wolsey's fall (see Guy, *The Cardinal's Court*, 15, 23–6, 51), and dividing by the number of remaining years in the reign. This method is somewhat arbitrary, but gives the reader some idea of the flow of cases. More precise figures await further research.

51 Hoak, *The King's Council in the Reign of Edward VI*, 222–28, 342–43.

52 This figure was obtained by dividing the number of extant suits for the reign by the number of years. See above, p. 20.

53 Skelton, 'The Court of Star Chamber in the Reign of Queen Elizabeth', Part 1, pp. 196–97.

54 Barnes, 'Star Chamber Litigants and their Counsel, 1596–1641', 8–9. I have again divided the number of suits filed in Star Chamber by the number of years of the reign.

55 Guy, *The Cardinal's Court*, 119–31.

56 Guy, *The Public Career of Sir Thomas More*, 80–93.

57 S. E. Lehmberg, 'Sir Thomas Audley: A Soul as Black as Marble?', in A. J. Slavin (*ed.*), *Tudor Men and Institutions* (Baton Rouge, 1972), 3–31.

58 Hoak, *The King's Council in the Reign of Edward VI*, 43–5, 231–58, 346 n. 18.

59 Lord Campbell, *Lives of the Lord Chancellors and Keepers of the Great Seal of England* (London, 5th ed. 1896), ii. 136–170.

60 Lemasters, 'The Privy Council in the Reign of Queen Mary I', 65.

61 PC 2/1, p. 43; N. H. Nicolas (*ed.*), *Proceedings and Ordinances of the Privy Council of England, 1368–*

1542 (7 vols., London, 1834–7), vii. 51–2, 112; *LP* xvi. 427, 465. See also D. A. Knox, 'The Court of Requests in the Reign of Edward VI' (Cambridge Ph.D. thesis, unpublished. 1974), 105, 108–10. Masters of requests were active in the task of sorting and preferring of petitions even after the abolition of the court of Requests, see *C.S.P.D., 1665–6*, p. 575.

62 C 82/945/33; *C.P.R., 1550–1553*, p. 353.

63 Hoak, *The King's Council in the Reign of Edward VI*, 222–23.

64 *Ibid.*

65 Pollard, 'Council, Star Chamber, and Privy Council under the Tudors', 337–60, 516–39; A.L. Brown, *The Early History of the Clerkship of the Council* (Glasgow University Publications N.S. 131, 1969).

66 *LP* i. I. 1462 (26); *LP* iv. III. 6490; Bayne and Dunham, *Select Cases in the Council of Henry VII*, lxxviii–lxxx; B.L. Hargrave MS. 216, fos. 103ᵛ–127ᵛ; Skelton, 'The Court of Star Chamber in the Reign of Queen Elizabeth', Part 1, pp. 42–44.

67 Pollard, 'Council, Star Chamber, and Privy Council under the Tudors', 337–60, 516–39.

68 *LP* ii. I. 1857; Pollard, 'Council, Star Chamber, and Privy Council under the Tudors', 347; S. E. Lehmberg, *Sir Thomas Elyot* (Austin, 1964), 27–9. Lehmberg is, however, incorrect when he states that Elyot held the senior clerkship. Richard Eden remained senior clerk until May 1530.

69 Lehmberg, *Sir Thomas Elyot*, 28.

70 B.L. Hargrave MS. 216, fo. 127ᵛ.

71 *LP* iv. II. 4231; Lehmberg, *Sir Thomas Elyot*, 29.

72 Lehmberg, *Sir Thomas Elyot*, 27–8.

73 B.L. Hargrave MS. 216, fo. 104ᵛ.

74 *LP* iv. III. 6490.

75 Lee's hand disappears from the

Star Chamber records early in More's chancellorship. Elyot continued his work (see STAC 2/3/ 219, 10/263–64, 13/64–68, 15/66, 93), but was 'discharged withoute any recompence' from his post under More's authority. Lehmberg, *Sir Thomas Elyot*, 28.

76 B.L. Hargrave MS. 216, fo. 127^v.

77 Richard Eden's hand disappears from the Star Chamber records at this point. He retired to Sudbury, where he was warden of the college of St. Gregory. He surrendered the college to the Crown on 9 December 1544. He died about April 1551.

78 *LP* xiii. II, p. 528; Elton, *The Tudor Revolution in Government*, 335, 441–2.

79 STAC 2/13/30–46, 2/13/183–86, 178–81, 2/14/1, 2/15/32–33, 2/15/ 188–90, 2/22/314, 2/26/103, 2/22/ 314; STAC 10/4, Pt. 2, fos. 127–32, 316–27, 347–48, 356–57; STAC 10/ 4, Pt. 5, fo. 21; SP 1/231, Pt. 3, fo. 287 (*LP Add.* 160); SP 1/234, Pt. 1, fos. 66–67 (*LP Add.* 422); SP 1/45, fo. 311 (*LP* iv. II. 3719); SP 1/16, fos. 141–43 (*LP* ii. II. 3951).

80 B.L. Hargrave MS. 216, fo. 130; B.L. Lansdowne MS. 639, fo. 58; H.E.H. Ellesmere MS. 2652, fo. 3^v.

81 H.E.H. Ellesmere MS. 2652, fo. 11^v.

82 However, the clerk had sometimes taken examinations under Henry VII, see STAC 10/8, fos. 393–94.

83 Skelton, 'The Court of Star Chamber in the Reign of Queen Elizabeth', Part 1, pp. 44–65.

84 STAC 10/4, Pt. 2, fos. 316–27, 347–50, 356–57; STAC 10/18, unfoliated (formerly Miscellanea B, no. 2); SP 1/231, Pt. 1, fos. 95–7 (*LP Add.* 64).

85 Skelton, 'The Court of Star Chamber in the Reign of Queen Elizabeth', Part 1, pp. 46–9; Barnes, 'The Archives and Archival Problems of the Elizabethan and Early Stuart Star Chamber', 346–48.

86 B.L. Additional MS. 37045, fo. 40^v; Skelton, 'The Court of Star Chamber in the Reign of Queen Elizabeth', Part 1, p. 47.

87 STAC 5/P. 4/28 (endorsement on bill of complaint); Skelton, 'The Court of Star Chamber in the Reign of Queen Elizabeth', Part 1, p. 48; Barnes, 'The Archives and Archival Problems of the Elizabethan and Early Stuart Star Chamber', 358. Congestion in Star Chamber itself was exacerbated by the fact that the 'outer' room was used for meetings of committees of the House of Commons from 1563 to 1597. See *The House of Commons, 1558–1603*, ed. P. W. Hasler (3 vols. London, 1981), i. 71, 75, 79, 82, 89, 93, 96.

88 Skelton, 'The Court of Star Chamber in the Reign of Queen Elizabeth', Part 1, pp. 48–9, 51–2.

89 B.L. Hargrave MS. 216, fo. 193.

90 Skelton, 'The Court of Star Chamber in the Reign of Queen Elizabeth', Part 1, p. 48. Edward Mills was acting as an examiner in 1596; STAC 10/18, fos. 40–1. Richard Robinson mentions one 'Mr. Linton' as an examiner. See 'A Briefe Collection of the Queenes Majesties Most High and Most Honourable Courtes of Records,' *Camden Miscellany*, 3rd series, lxxxiii (London, 1953), 22.

91 Skelton, 'The Court of Star Chamber in the Reign of Queen Elizabeth', Part 1, p. 49. Robinson says Thomas Mills occupied it in 1592 (p. 22).

92 *Ibid.* Thomas Underwood held the post.

93 Skelton, 'The Court of Star Chamber in the Reign of Queen Elizabeth', Part 1, pp. 51–2. The first incumbent was Richard Dallidown.

94 B.L. Hargrave MS. 216, fos. 187^v–

194^v; H.E.H. Ellesmere MSS. 2669, 2676, 2680; Skelton, 'The Court of Star Chamber in the Reign of Queen Elizabeth', Part 1, pp. 51–63; Barnes, 'The Archives and Archival Problems of the Elizabethan and Early Stuart Star Chamber', 346–49.

95 H.E.H. Ellesmere MS. 2680.

96 B.L. Hargrave MS. 216, fos. 192^v–194^v.

97 *Ibid.*, fos. 184^v–192^v; B.L. Lansdowne MS. 639, fos. 17^v–21^v; B.L. Stowe MS. 418, fos. 117–131; B.L. Additional MS. 26647, fos. 216–220; Barnes, 'Due Process and Slow Process in the late Elizabethan–early Stuart Star Chamber', 221–49, 315–46.

98 H.E.H. Ellesmere MSS. 2676–77; J. P. Collier (*ed.*), *The Egerton Papers* (London, Camden Society, 1840), 316–17.

99 B.L. Lansdowne MS. 639, fo. 21; B.L. Harleian MS. 2310; Skelton, 'The Court of Star Chamber in the Reign of Queen Elizabeth', Part 1, p. 54, and appendix.

100 Barnes, 'The Archives and Archival Problems of the Elizabethan and Early Stuart Star Chamber', 346–49; Barnes, 'Mr. Hudson's Star Chamber', in *Tudor Rule and Revolution*, ed. DeLloyd J. Guth and J. W. McKenna (Cambridge, 1982), 285–308.

101 C 82/661; *LP* v. 1499 (8).

102 C 82/661.

103 C 66/664, m. 33; *LP* vii. 1601 (33).

104 Skelton, 'The Court of Star Chamber in the Reign of Queen Elizabeth', Part 1, pp. 50–1.

105 *Ibid.*; Barnes, 'The Archives and Archival Problems of the Elizabethan and Early Stuart Star Chamber', 346–47.

106 STAC 8/93/8 (formerly STAC 5/C. 98/8).

107 SP 46/123, fo. 124; *LP* iv. II. 3087.

108 B.L. Harleian MS. 1226, fo. 14.

109 B.L. Lansdowne MS. 639, fo. 20; H.E.H. Ellesmere MS. 2676.

110 Access to the records was a potential cause of friction: H.E.H. Ellesmere MS. 2669; Barnes, 'The Archives and Archival Problems of the Elizabethan and Early Stuart Star Chamber', 358–59.

111 B.L. Hargrave MS. 216, fos. 191^v–192^v; B.L. Harleian MS. 1220, fo. 121^v.

112 B.L. Hargrave MS. 216, fo. 127^v; B.L. Harleian MS. 1220, fo. 121^v.

113 H.E.H. Ellesmere MS. 2652, fo. 3^v.

114 B.L. Hargrave MS. 216, fo. 130; B.L. Lansdowne MS. 639, fo. 58; H.E.H. Ellesmere MS. 2652, fo. 3^v.

115 STAC 10/4, Pt. 2, fos. 316–27; STAC 2/17/397.

116 STAC 2/44/155.

117 B.L. Hargrave MS. 216, fo. 108.

118 Barnes, 'Mr. Hudson's Star Chamber', 301.

119 STAC 2/17/397; STAC 2/33/43; STAC 10/4, Pt. 2, fos. 316–27; STAC 3/6/106; STAC 4/8/4, 33, 53; B.L. Harleian MS. 1200, fo. 121^v; B.L.Hargrave MS. 216, fo. 127^v; STAC 5/B. 4/27; STAC 5/B. 5/6; STAC 5/E. 5/34; STAC 5/S. 33/7; STAC 5/F. 1/15; H.E.H. Ellesmere MSS. 2669, 2676; Skelton, 'The Court of Star Chamber in the Reign of Queen Elizabeth', Part 1, p. 64.

120 H.E.H. Ellesmere MS. 2655, fo. 12^v; Skelton, 'The Court of Star Chamber in the Reign of Queen Elizabeth', Part 1, p. 53; Robinson, p.22.

121 Baldwin, *The King's Council in England during the Middle Ages*, 358–62.

122 Skelton, 'The Court of Star Chamber in the Reign of Queen Elizabeth', Part 1, pp. 52–3.

123 C. L. Scofield, 'Accounts of Star Chamber Dinners, 1593–4', *American Historical Review*, v (1899), 85–95.

Chapter 2 Star Chamber Records to 1558

1 Barnes, 'The Archives and Archival Problems of the Elizabethan and Early Stuart Star Chamber', 357–60.

2 *Ibid.* The same report was repeated in 1719. *Journals of the House of Lords*, xxi. 137. A modern search failed to discover the site of the house, which may have been confused with that of the Cotton family (see above, p. 15). E. A. Webb, *The Records of St. Bartholomew's Priory and the Church and Parish of St. Bartholomew the Great West Smithfield* (Oxford, 1921), ii. 283.

3 *Journals of the House of Lords*, xxi. 142.

4 These bundles are appended to STAC 2/28, box 2; 2/29, box 2; 2/30, box 2; 2/31, box 2; 2/32, box 2.

5 Appendix D identifies Star Chamber cases in STAC 10 belonging to the reigns of Henry VII, Henry VIII, Edward VI, Philip and Mary, and Elizabeth I. It also notes some Requests and Chancery cases to 1603 wrongly placed in STAC 10.

6 See above, appendices A and D.

7 Two suits of Wolsey's chancellorship were found to have documents in no fewer than seven different bundles. *Abbot of Ford* v. *Poyntz*, STAC 2/15/159, 17/259, 19/305, 20/7, 24/67, 25/203, 31/loose paper (bundle of unlisted fragments); *Sweteman* v. *Brereton*, STAC 2/3/311, 17/227, 185, 18/162, 19/81, 22/113, 24/434, 26/370.

8 See above, appendix A.

9 See above, appendix A.

10 See above, appendix D.

11 The minutes of the clerks of the Council for Henry VIII's reign have been placed mostly in STAC 10/4, Pt. 2. The returned writs for the reign of Philip and Mary are in STAC 10/20, Pt. 2. STAC 10/20, Pt. 1 contains writs of Elizabeth I's reign. The regnal years represented in STAC 10/20, Pt. 2 are 1 and 2, and 4 Philip and Mary.

12 See above, pp. 25–28.

13 See above, p. 7.

14 B.L. Hargrave MS. 216, fo. 119^v.

15 E.g. SP 1/16, fos. 35–6 (*LP* ii. II. 3741); SP 1/19, fos. 88–91 (*LP* iii. II. App. 5); SP 1/234, fos. 66–7 (*LP Add.* 422); SP 1/46, fos. 251–52 (*LP* iv. II. 3926), printed in *Bulletin of the Institute of Historical Research*, v (1927), 23–27; SP 1/16, fos. 140–43 (*LP* ii. II. 3951); SP 1/231, fos. 95–7 (*LP Add.* 64); SP 1/45, fo. 51 (*LP* iv. II. 3579); SP 1/17, fos. 248–49 (*LP* ii. II. App. 60), which resembles STAC 2/25/214.

16 E.g. SP 1/45, fos. 311–12 (*LP* iv. II. 3719); SP 1/236, fo. 153 (*LP Add.* 661); SP 1/34, fos. 5–8 (*LP* iv. I. 1115); SP 1/55, fos. 240–41 (*LP* iv. III. 6028); SP 1/236, fos. 45–6 (*LP Add.* 624).

17 E.g. SP 1/19, fos. 143–44 (*LP* iii. I. 571); SP 1/21, fos. 144–58 (*LP* iii. I. 1113); SP 1/29, fos. 236–90 (*LP* iii. II. App. 12); SP 1/32, fos. 70–1 (*LP* iv. I. 655); SP 1/37, fos. 65–103 (*LP* iv. I. 1939); SP 1/45, fo. 51 (*LP* iv. II. 3579); SP 1/46, fo. 199 (*LP* iv. II. 3864); SP 1/58, fos. 150–51 (*LP* iv. III. 6708); SP 1/59, fo. 77 (*LP* iv. III. App. 67); SP 1/233, fo. 274 (*LP Add.* 402); SP 1/235, fo. 37 (*LP Add.* 481); SP 1/235, fos. 74–6 (*LP Add.* 501); SP 1/235, fo. 100 (*LP Add.* 511); SP 1/235, fos. 109–19 (*LP Add.* 516); SP 1/236, fos. 66–71 (*LP Add.* 642); B.L. Cotton MS. Vespasian F. xiii, fo. 234 (*LP* iii. I. 873); *LP* iii. II. 2415; *LP* iv. I. 1136 (22); B.L. Additional MS. 5949 (*LP* iv. I. 1366).

18 E.g. SP 1/11, fo. 82 (*LP* ii. I. 911); *LP* ii. I. 1861, 1870, 2018; SP 1/16, fos. 15–16 (*LP* ii. II. App. 38); SP 1/18, fos. 155–56 (*LP* iii. I. 207);

LP iii. I. 356; SP 1/22, fo. 208 (*LP*
iii. I. 1374); SP 1/23, fo. 227 (*LP*
iii. II. 1923); SP 1/26, fos. 150–51
(*LP* iii. II. 2653); *LP* iv. I. 705; SP
1/34, fos. 41–2 (*LP* iv. I. 1156); SP
1/36, fo. 98 (*LP* iv. I. 2076); SP
1/39, fos. 163–64 (*LP* iv. II. 2521);
SP 1/42, fos. 61–4 (*LP* iv. II. 3154);
SP 1/47, fos. 38–9 (*LP* iv. II. 3997);
SP 1/47, fos. 224–25 (*LP* iv. II.
4148); SP 1/53, fos. 186–87 (*LP* iv.
III. 5430); SP 1/53, fo. 200 (*LP* iv.
III. 5460); SP 1/57, fos. 179–84
(*LP* iv. III. 6467); SP 1/59, fo. 127
(*LP* iv. III. App. 176); *LP* iv. III.
App. 207; SP 1/59, fos. 149–50 (*LP*
iv. III. App. 242).
19 C 244/138–182; C 263/3.
20 E.g. E 208/19 (Star Chamber
    decree).
21 E.g. E 401/958 (Star Chamber
    fines).
22 E.g. C 66/627, mm. 13–14; E 315/
    313A, fos. 43ᵛ–44 (Star Chamber
    decrees). For Star Chamber fines
    on Exchequer Memoranda rolls,
    see below n. 101.
23 E 407/51.
24 SP 1/33, fos. 203–85 (*LP* iv. I.
    1097). See also B.L. Lansdowne
    MS. 1, fos. 136–40; Folger
    Shakespeare Library, Washington
    D.C., MS. V.b. 179.
25 E 36/215, 216, under 'Obligations'.
    See also, B.L. Additional MS.
    21481. For comparative purposes,
    see E 101/414/16, fos. 214, 251,
    259.
26 Barnes, 'The Archives and Archival
    Problems of the Elizabethan and
    Early Stuart Star Chamber', 356–7.
27 The dates of appointment of lord
    chancellors are listed in *Handbook
    of British Chronology*, ed. F. M.
    Powicke and E. B. Fryde (London,
    Royal Historical Society. 2nd ed.,
    1961), 86–7.
28 The full form of words ran thus:
    *Vocentur Ricardus Crippes et
    Edwardus Chamberleyn per brevem
    de sub pena* (or *de privato sigillo*, or

very rarely *per litteras missivas*) *ad
comparendum coram domino Rege et
consilio suo apud Westmonasterium in
crastino Animarum sub pena
cuiuslibet eorum Centum librarum.
Ex decreto et mandato domini
cancellarii* (or *dominorum consilii*) *xij
die Octobris.* E.g. STAC 2/4/58, 12/
221, 13/241, 15/76, 26/189.
29 For the handwriting of Robert
    Rydon, see B.L. Cotton MS.
    Vespasian F. xiii, fo. 145ᵛ (note
    addressed to 'oon of the clerkes of
    the previseale in hast'). See also
    Bayne and Dunham, *Select Cases in
    the Council of Henry VII*, xx, lxxix–
    lxxx, lxxxiii–lxxxviii, xcvi, cv–cvi,
    clxii, 33, 114, 125. For that of
    Thomas Elyot, see clerical material
    upon cases in STAC 2/3/181, 219,
    276; 4/228; 5/138, 149–50, 167–68;
    7/23, 120, 137; 8/137, 215–17; 9/
    138–48; 10/72–82, 111, 121, 216–
    21, 263–64; 13/48–50A, 64–8; 15/
    66, 75, 93, 281–82; 16/190–96; 17/
    160, 189, 253, 401; 18/71; 19/90,
    370; 20/400; 21/17, 22, 30, 90, 230;
    22/84; 23/73; 25/336; 26/189, 209,
    235; 27/47, 50, 108, 170; 28/19, 32,
    52, 67; 29/17, 47, 78, 125, 141,
    loose paper (bundle of unlisted
    fragments); 30/56, 115; 31/53, 94,
    100, 118, 155, 177; 32/18, 27. For
    handwriting of Richard Lee, see
    clerical material upon cases in
    STAC 2/1/154–58, 160; 2/134, 150,
    178–182; 3/1–2; 4/58, 59A–61; 6/
    170–75; 7/143–44, 207–8; 8/134–
    35; 9/45, 159; 10/16–19, 21, 41,
    131–32; 11/17–25, 87; 12/93–5,
    186, 221–4; 13/81–2, 138, 204, 241;
    15/34, 270–71; 16/20–2, 35, 190–6;
    17/80, 172, 211, 389; 18/99, 165,
    290, 302; 19/193, 198, 218; 20/143,
    328, 363; 21/19, 71, 135, 138, 139,
    192, 199, 200, 229, 235, 239; 22/50;
    23/54, 63, 77, 97, 150, 153, 179,
    222, 236, 270, 307, 319; 25/333; 26/
    345; 28/42, 108; 29/40, 50; 30/80,
    109, 114; 31/5, 12, 23, 36, 70; 32/
    81, 82; 33/13, 41; 35/11, 13, 65.

30 See his clerical material upon cases in STAC 2/5/138; 7/143–44; 12/150–53, 158–59, 221–24; 13/30–46, 178–81, 183–86; 14/1; 15/32–3, 34, 188–90; 21/199, 200, 229, 235, 239; 22/314, 328; 25/8, 172; 26/103, 201; 27/110; 28/8, 68; 29/loose paper (bundle of unlisted fragments); 30/52; 32/107; STAC 10/4, Pt. 2, fos. 316–27 (Richard Eden's is the predominant hand in this pocket-book).

31 For the handwriting of Thomas Eden, see clerical material upon STAC 2/1/183–86; 12/143–44; 19/178, 273, 321–22; 20/58, 270; 21/117; 23/244; 28/71.

32 I have not traced this order, but the impact of changed procedure in this year can be seen in the records, e.g. STAC 4/8/53, 54, 55, 56, 57, 58, 59, 60, 61, 62 (all 'K' plaintiffs in 1556).

33 See above, pp. 29–35

34 We know from the Ellesmere MSS. at the Huntington Library and *Libri Intrationum* at the British Library, for instance, that about 213 Star Chamber cases were heard during Wolsey's chancellorship for which no proceedings can now be found in STAC 2 or 10.

35 The Elizabethan endorsements are in a distinctive hand in the extreme corners of bills. They note the surnames of the principal parties; such work was perhaps connected with the compilation of calendars of records by William Mill. See H.E.H. Ellesmere MS. 2680. Official evidence of the Elizabethan work is to be found in the note upon E 163/10/28B.

36 No other documents carry the Elizabethan endorsements. That the archive remained generally disorganized is apparent from H.E.H. Ellesmere MSS. 2678, 2680.

37 See above, appendices B, C, D for pre-1558 cases in STAC 2 and 10

belonging to Requests and Chancery.

38 For examples of the handwriting of pre-1558 clerks of the Council, see references listed above, nn. 29–31. For a Star Chamber order of 30 November 1584, subscribed by Thomas Marshe (clerk from 1567 to 1587), see STAC 10/18, fo. 47.

39 That is, *coram consilio nostro apud Westmonasterium*, or 'we wyll that ye certifie us and our Counsell in the sterr chamber at Westminster' in the case of a *dedimus potestatem* in English.

40 See pre-1558 examples in REQ 3/1–10.

41 E.g. C 1/601–94 (documents of More's chancellorship).

42 STAC 2/1/35.

43 That is, eschewing.

44 That is, county.

45 That is, encouraging.

46 Utter-barrister. The plaintiff's counsel was required to subscribe his name to bills of complaint by the end of Henry VIII's reign, though signatures are sometimes found earlier.

47 Guy, *The Cardinal's Court*, 53–9.

48 For the common law background, see S. F. C. Milsom, *Historical Foundations of the Common Law* (London, 1969), 127–39; A. W. B. Simpson, *An Introduction to the History of the Land Law* (Oxford, 1961), 34–43.

49 ASSI 16/34/3 (bigamy at Great Shelford, Cambs., the second marriage celebrated *vi et armis* in the village church).

50 Claimants to real property who mustered a following and took possession, but who were repulsed by sitting tenants and their servants, alleged in Star Chamber, after the former fashion of *novel disseisin* at common law, that they themselves had been put out by armies of 'riotous' persons, while 'seised in their demesne as of

freehold'. E.g. *Frechewell* v. *Lowe*, STAC 2/19/27; *Heed* v. *Franke*, STAC 2/19/198.

51 E.g. *Agarde* v. *Corbet*, STAC 2/1/36–7; *Cantrell* v. *Tatton*, STAC 2/24/26, 18/326; *Curwen* v. *Belyngeham*, STAC 2/11/104–29; *Percey* v. *Somervyle*, STAC 2/35/58; *Bayly* v. *Wallope*, STAC 2/20/309, 334, 17/45, 19/388.

52 See the remarks by J. A. Guy, 'The Development of Equitable Jurisdictions, 1450–1550' in *Law, Litigants, and the Legal Profession*, ed. E. W. Ives and A. H. Manchester (London, Royal Historical Society, 1983), 80–6; Barnes 'Star Chamber Litigants and their Counsel, 1596–1641', 15–17.

53 Guy, *The Cardinal's Court*, 49, 81; W. J. Jones, *The Elizabethan Court of Chancery* (Oxford, 1967), 314–7.

54 STAC 4/11/44.

55 Jones, *The Elizabethan Court of Chancery*, 214.

56 B.L. Hargrave MS. 216, fo. 128^v; B.L. Lansdowne MS. 639, fo. 1; Bayne and Dunham, *Select Cases in the Council of Henry VII*, lxxi.

57 Bayne and Dunham, *Select Cases in the Council of Henry VII*, ciii.

58 See above, pp. 56–60.

59 Guy, *The Cardinal's Court*, 51–8.

60 Replications and rejoinders none the less continued at ever increasing length, perhaps because the court's officers had a vested interest in the fees that accrued from filing and copying them.

61 Baldwin, *The King's Council in England during the Middle Ages*, 529–31; N. Adams and C. Donahue (*eds.*), *Select Cases from the Ecclesiastical Courts of the Province of Canterbury, c. 1200–1301* (London, Selden Society, 1981), introduction pp. *43–56*.

62 B.L. Lansdowne MS. 639, fo. 1.

63 The usual form was as follows: 'John Smith clerk of Great Shelford

in the county of Cambridge aged xxx years and more sworn the xxij day of November in the xxxth year of king Henry the viijth'.

64 See above, pp. 43–5.

65 E.g. H.E.H. Ellesmere MS. 2652, fos. 10^v, 17^v, 18^v. Guy, *The Cardinal's Court*, 17, 18–19, 20, 25, 34, 52–3, 61–2, 73, 75, 77, 87, 117, 126. It was eventually settled that perjury in Chancery was examinable in Star Chamber even when the suit in Chancery remained undetermined. *Dennys* v. *Rolle*, STAC 8/115/10.

66 These items were collected as much as anything in the quest for precedents affirming Star Chamber's jurisdiction, which Egerton was anxious to defend.

67 A calendar of the Ellesmere MSS. is available in the Cambridge University Library (Microfilms 771–2). A few Star Chamber documents were printed in *The Egerton Papers*, ed. J. P. Collier (London, Camden Society, 1840).

68 E.g. the rough lists of precedents in H.E.H. Ellesmere MSS. 479, 2757, in Egerton's hand are compiled from H.E.H. Ellesmere MSS. 2654–55. The marginal additions in H.E.H. Ellesmere 2655, in Egerton's hand, are at fos. 12, 14^v.

69 Henry VIII material begins on fo. 22^v and ends on fo. 25. Henry VII material is printed in Bayne and Dunham, *Select Cases in the Council of Henry VII*, 6–47.

70 The scribal errors, e.g. fos. 13, 18, are not commensurate with an attempt at a fair copy. The paper used, which is French, bears a distinctive watermark of the type Briquet no. 14038 (1593).

71 H.E.H. Ellesmere MS. 2768 is not a 'volume' proper, but a series of leaves of various sizes later bound together. Thereafter more loose leaves were inserted from elsewhere in the Ellesmere collection. The

final result was foliated as if it were a single manuscript.

72 B.L. Hargrave MS. 216, fo. 100. See also W. H. Dunham, 'The Ellesmere Extracts from the *Acta Consilii* of King Henry VIII', *English Historical Review*, lviii (1943), 301–18. Dunham's paper was, however, written without the benefit of a sight of the Public Record Office materials. It is clear from a note on fo. 57 that H.E.H. Ellesmere MS. 2768 was in preparation at the latest by 1577.

73 B.L. Hargrave MS. 216, fos. 130–80.

74 *Ibid.*, fo. 100.

75 H.E.H. Ellesmere MS. 2655, fo. 18^v.

76 B.L. Lansdowne MS. 160, fo. 311^v.

77 E.g. STAC 10/4, Pt. 2, fos. 356–7; 10/4, Pt. 2, fos. 347–8; 10/4, Pt. 2, fos. 316–27; SP 1/231, fo. 287.

78 The extent to which the columns flanked the page in Eden's work naturally depended on the size of the attendance. On days when the presence was small, the parallel columns appeared less widely spaced, immediately above the *acta*, and beneath the word '*presentibus*'. See Eden's drafts in STAC 10/4, Pt. 2, fos. 316–27. 10/4, Pt. 2, fo. 356 contains the parallel columns of names, but no *acta*. Evidently nothing worthy of note was decided.

79 H.E.H. Ellesmere MS. 2655, fos. 11^v, 16, which contain two entries in Latin are exceptional. The decree in *Buckenham* v. *Clyff*, STAC 2/7/17–19, 35/30, is in Latin, but this draft was prepared by counsel, not by a clerk of the Council.

80 H.E.H. Ellesmere MS. 2655, fos. 12^v–13; STAC 2/1/96.

81 2 May 1516: H.E.H. Ellesmere MS. 2655, fo. 10; STAC 10/18, document formerly marked

Miscellany B (bundle 2). 20 February 1517: H.E.H. Ellesmere MS. 2655, fo. 11; STAC 2/15/117–18. 14 October 1518: H.E.H. Ellesmere MS. 2655, fo. 13; STAC 2/15/114–15. 6 November 1518: H.E.H. Ellesmere MS. 2655, fo. 14; STAC 2/2/75.

82 The manuscript has not been provided with modern foliation, and all references are to Egerton's own foliation in which fo. 1 is the first page of precedents and not the first leaf.

83 See above, p. 34.

84 H.E.H. Ellesmere MSS. 485, 495, 2653, 2656, 2657, 2658, 2659, 2757 (fo. 1), 2766.

85 H.E.H. Ellesmere MSS. 479, 2757 (fo. 2), 2768 (former loose leaves now fos. 31–40), 2810.

86 Cf. H.E.H. Ellesmere MS. 2652.

87 H.E.H. Ellesmere MSS. 2669, 2676, 2678, 2680, 2683.

88 B.L. Additional MS. 4521, fos. 104^v–151^v. B.L. Hargrave MS. 216, fos. 145–57, which is in part a copy of H.E.H. Ellesmere MS. 2768, fos. 1–25, but the copy was evidently made before the leaves of the Ellesmere MS. became disordered.

89 B.L. Additional MS. 4521, fos. 120–151^v.

90 See also London Guildhall MS. 1751, pp. 199–250; Corpus Christi College Oxford MS. 196, pp. 116–56; Bodleian Library MS. Eng. hist. c. 304, fos. 317a–346^v.

91 Hudson's work was done during the period 1618–1621.

92 See above, appendix E.

93 B.L. Lansdowne MS. 639, fo. 23.

94 *Ibid.*, fo. 99^v.

95 STAC 2/1/96; B.L. Lansdowne MS. 639, fo. 54. SP 1/34, fos. 5–8 (*LP* iv. I. 1115); B.L. Lansdowne MS. 639, fos. 56^v–7. STAC 2/13/204; B.L. Lansdowne MS. 639, fo. 57. H.E.H. Ellesmere MS. 2655, fos. 7–8; B.L. Lansdowne MS.

639, fo. 28. H.E.H. Ellesmere MS. 2655, fos. 8ᵛ–9; B.L. Lansdowne MS. 639, fos. 34–5. H.E.H. Ellesmere MS. 2655, fo. 16ᵛ; B.L. Lansdowne MS. 639, fo. 56.

96 B.L. Lansdowne MS. 639, fos. 23ᵛ–59.

97 *Ibid.*, fos. 28, 36–7, 46ᵛ, 58ᵛ.

98 *Ibid.*, fos. 28, 33, 34ᵛ, 40ᵛ, 44ᵛ, 45, 46ᵛ, 47, 48ᵛ, 49.

99 *Ibid.*, fos. 39, 49ᵛ–52ᵛ.

100 Barnes, 'The Archives and Archival Problems of the Elizabethan and Early Stuart Star Chamber', 356.

101 E 159/334 Rec. Mich. rot. 225; 335 Rec. Hil. rot. 106; 337 Rec. Mich. rot. 165, Hil. rot. 134; 338 Rec. Mich. rot. 157, Hil. rot. 109, Trin. rot. 53 (dorse); 339 Rec. Mich. rot. 110. I owe these references to the kindness of Dr. Michael Zell.

102 B.L. Lansdowne MS. 160, fos. 307–13.

Chapter 3 Star Chamber Procedure to 1558

1 See above, pp. 25–7.

2 The origins of the form may be discerned in the petition of John Harpetyn to the King's Council filed about 1398. See Baldwin, *The King's Council in England during the Middle Ages*, 520–1.

3 STAC 2/16/365–72; 17/437; 23/24; 32/97; 33/44.

4 STAC 2/18/153, 234; 21/84, 158.

5 STAC 2/2/156–7, 158, 161–2, 163, 167–9, 170, 171–3, 174–6, 176–77, 178–82, 183–7, 190–3, 194–7, 197–203, 205, 206–9, 210–16, 217–20; STAC 3/6/69, 71; STAC 4/3/41, 43, 46, 58, 59, 62, 63, 66, 72; 8/1, 4, 12, 13, 14, 16, 17, 18.

6 The procedure followed by the mature court of Star Chamber was outlined thus: 'When a delinquent is examined by some of the kinges learned Counsell, Judges or others for a criminall matter punishable in this Court, And shall confesse the matter, he is brought to the bar, and there allso if he shall confesse, his hand subscribed and that to be his examinacion, Then the Court proceedeth to sentence him upon that his confession without the former way of pleadinges and proofes, for it needeth not when his owne mouth hath condempned him allreadie' (B.L. Lansdowne MS. 639, fo. 15).

7 STAC 2/1/100, 101, 102, 103, 104, 105, 106, 107, 108, 109, 110, 111, 112, 113–26, 127, 128, 129; STAC 3/6/60, 61, 65, 66, 70, 73, 74; STAC 4/3/40, 44, 45, 47, 48, 50, 57, 60, 67, 70, 73; 8/5, 19, 20, 22.

8 Guy, *The Cardinal's Court*, 80–2.

9 More's concern to curtail the practice in Chancery is described by Guy, *The Public Career of Sir Thomas More*, 89–93. Egerton noted that in Henry VII's reign: 'the plaintiff was comenly bounde, and somtyme with suerties, to prove his pleynt or to paye Costes' (H.E.H. Ellesmere MS. 2652, fo. 1ᵛ). Shortly after taking up office in 1596, he issued a general order that no *subpoena* was to be sued out of Star Chamber before a bill was filed of record. However, the reform did not last. 'But divers inconveniences being found to happen thereby aswell to the suitor as otherwise, It hath sithence beene and is the use to take out Subpoenas without a Bill, and to file the Bill upon the Returne thereof' (B.L. Lansdowne MS. 639, fo. 1ᵛ).

10 The 'first and ould course' of Star Chamber was 'That the plaintiff shall upon his perill have his Bill perfect and on the file by or before the last day of the Returne of the Subpoena' (B.L. Lansdowne MS. 639, fo. 1ᵛ).

11 B.L. Lansdowne MS. 639, fos. 41ᵛ, 44ᵛ. Wolsey issued a general order on 12 June 1529 that 'if the

plaintiffs bille be not redy the next
daye after the deff[endant]s
apparance the deffs to be dismissed
with Costes, and the Clerke of the
Counsell to taxe the Costes in
absence of the L. Chancellor'
(H.E.H. Ellesmere MS. 2652, fo.
11^v).

12 H.E.H. Ellesmere MS. 2655, fo.
17^v; B.L. Lansdowne MS. 639, fos.
49, 57^v.

13 H.E.H. Ellesmere MS. 2655, fos.
13^v, 14; H.E.H. Ellesmere MS.
2652, fos. 2, 6^v; SP 1/46, fo. 252
(*LP* iv. II. 3926); STAC 10/4, Pt.
2, fos. 338–9.

14 Guy, *The Cardinal's Court*, 82–3.

15 The form of words might be
standard or adapted to suit special
circumstances. A form adapted to
riot in 1503 read: 'For certain great
Riottes and misgovernaunces late
by you and every of you committed
and doon within oure Countie of
Berk contrary to oure lawes and
peas as we be enformed we wol and
straitly charge you that almaner
excuses and dilaies utterly laide
apart ye and every of you be and
personally apper afor us and our
Counsaill at oure Palois of
Westminster in the xv^{ine} of pasche
next commyng to aunswere to the
said Riottes and suche othre thinges
as at your commyng shalbe laide
and objected ayenst you w[ithout]
failing herof upon payne every of
you of C li and as ye wol aunswere
untu us at your further p[eril]
yeven undre our prive Seal at oure
manor of Richemount the 18 day of
February'. Bayne and Dunham,
*Select Cases in the Council of Henry
VII*, lxxxvii.

16 Of 139 cases filed under Wolsey in
which the form of process issued is
stated, in 96 the defendants were
summoned by writs of *subpoena*.

17 The standard format was:
'Henricus octavus dei gracia Rex
Anglie et Francie fidei defensor et
dominus Hibernie Johanni Smith,
salutem. Quibusdam certis de
causis coram nobis et Consilio
nostro propositis, tibi precipimus
firmiter injungentes, quod omnibus
aliis pretermissis et excusacione
quacumque cessante, in propria
persona tua sis coram nobis et
Consilio nostro in quindena pasche
proximo futura sine ulteriori
dilacione, ad respondendum
ibidem super hiis quae tunc tibi
obicientur, et ad faciendum ulterius
et recipiendum quod per nos et
dictum Consilium nostrum tunc
ibidem contigerit ordinari. Et hoc
sub pena Centum librarum
nullatenus omittas. Et habeas ibi
hoc breve. Teste me ipso apud
Hampton Courte xxj die Marcii,
anno regni nostri decimo septimo'.
For an example of a special writ
adapted to suit a title dispute in
Wolsey's chancellorship, see STAC
2/18/319. Later returned examples
of Star Chamber writs of *subpoena*,
lacking the tickets, which were
mostly retained by the parties, are
found in STAC 10/20, Pts. 1–2.
STAC 10/20, Pt. 1 contains
Elizabethan writs; 10/20, Pt. 2
holds writs dated 1 and 2, and 4
Philip and Mary.

18 Legal chronology is fully explained
in *Handbook of Dates for Students of
English History*, ed. C. R. Cheney
(London, Royal Historical Society,
1970), 65–9. Return days were
those appointed for the return of all
writs issued since the last day of
return: *octavis* (the eighth day
after); *quindena* (the fifteenth day
after); *crastino* (the day after); *tres*
(three weeks after); *mense* (one
month after); *quinque* (five weeks
after). The Feast of St. Hilary is 13
January; the Purification, 2
February; Michaelmas, 29
September; *animarum
commemoratio* (All Soul's Day), 2
November; St. Martin's, 11

November; Easter (*Pascha*), Ascension Day, and Trinity Sunday are movable feasts.

19 B.L. Lansdowne MS. 639, fo. 25ᵛ.
20 STAC 2/4/98–108; 23/252; B.L. Lansdowne MS. 639, fo. 34.
21 STAC 10/4, Pt. 2, fos. 316–27.
22 See above, p. 27.
23 In the last resort, process of contempt leading to discretionary imprisonment would be invoked. The mature procedure of Star Chamber is described in B.L. Lansdowne MS. 639, fos. 2–5.
24 If a defendant made a plea in bar or demurred to the court's jurisdiction, he was not examined upon interrogatories as to the matter raised unless the plea was rejected by the court. He was sworn, however, to the truth of his plea.
25 The mature Star Chamber did not permit the welding of answers with demurrers or pleas in bar. B.L. Lansdowne MS. 639, fo. 4ᵛ.
26 John Waller claimed that his opponent's bill was determinable 'by the Course of the commen lawe and not elles where for asmoche as it touchith mannys liff' (STAC 2/24/25). He went on, nevertheless, to answer. For the statutory restrictions on Star Chamber's jurisdiction, see Guy, *The Cardinal's Court*, 14–15.
27 H.E.H. Ellesmere MS. 2680. In Mary's reign, Otes Hunt clerk and John Burton demurred on the grounds that they lived 140 miles from London, and that their case had arisen within the jurisdiction of the Council of the North, to which they prayed to be remitted (STAC 4/11/11). For a mature demurrer filed in 1617, see STAC 8/115/10. The defendants, being accused of perjury in Chancery, argued: 'It is against the course of this Courte and against the Justice of this Realme to examine in this moste

honorable Courte anie such periurie, subornation, or misdemeanore before the suite in which the same is supposed to bee committed shalbe fully heard and ended'. This plea was rejected.
28 See above, p. 27.
29 Thus on 3 February 1517, Thomas and James Bradford 'sworne and severally examined seyen and either of theym seith that as to any Riote forcible entre or other mysdemeanor supposed in the seid bill to be doon ayenst the kinges lawes or peace they be yn noo thyng giltye and all oth[er] thinges conteyned in this their answere they and either of theym afferme to be of trouthe Soo helpe theym God' (STAC 2/12/222).
30 For instance, Lord Slane's counsel filed on 22 November 1531, interrogatories for the examination of Patrick Bellowe and Robert Dyllon: 'Here folowith th'interrogatorys wheruppon Patrik Bellowe and Robert Dyllon shalbe examyned at the Sute of James Flemyng Baron of Slane' (STAC 2/20/347). There were five questions, a modest number in comparison with the dozens that had become customary by 1603. However, in Mary's reign three to five questions were still normal. On 13 October 1554, Henry Williams was examined upon the interrogatories of Jane Stourton before Thomas Eden, clerk of the Council in Star Chamber. There were two questions concerning title to a close occupied by Roger Stourton at the time of his death (STAC 4/11/60).
31 STAC 2/3/311; 17/185, 227; 18/162; 19/81; 20/363; 22/113, 276; 23/66; 24/153, 434; 26/370.
32 H.E.H. Ellesmere MS. 2652, fos. 10ᵛ, 17ᵛ, 18ᵛ.
33 B.L. Harleian MS. 2143, fos. 11–12.
34 Bayne and Dunham, *Select Cases in*

the Council of Henry VII, civ–vi; Guy, *The Cardinal's Court*, 87–9.

35 For affidavits taken in Star Chamber by the clerk of the Council in Trinity term 1525, see STAC 10/4, Pt. 2, fos. 325–6. For instance, 'William Tompkyn of th'age of xxvj [yeres] sworn this iiijth day of July sayth that Thomas Penworthy that hadd day to appere in octavis Johannis by virtue of a s[ub]p[ena] ys a man of lx & xvi yere olde & of suche Impotence that he may not ryde nor go witowt daunger of his lyfe to kepe his apparaunce here accordyng to effect of the same s[ub]p[ena].

36 STAC 2/21/56.

37 STAC 4/8/53.

38 STAC 2/14/113–15; 18/323; 25/2; 26/195, 197.

39 Guy, *The Cardinal's Court*, 97–105.

40 For background, see E. Powell, 'Arbitration and the Law in England in the Late Middle Ages', *Transactions of the Royal Historical Society*, 5th series, xxxiii (1983), 49–67.

41 See above, pp. 48–9.

42 This fact was noted by one of the compilers of the Ellesmere extracts: 'In the tyme of H. 8 untill the beginni[n]ge of Queene Elizab[eth] & for divers yeres in her Raigne also, It was very usuall in causes depending to graunte comissions to gentlemen in the Country to examine and finally to decide and determyne the controversies betweene the parties if they coulde or els to certifie unto the court; and theis comissions were then the usuall & most ordinary course which the court tooke for dispatch and ease of the Subiecte & the courte' (H.E.H. Ellesmere MS. 2658).

43 Examples cited from B.L. Lansdowne MS. 639, fo. 4. The second rule quoted was reversed in 1628 in *Apsley* v. *Ridley*.

44 STAC 10/4, Pt. 2, fos. 316–27.

45 B.L. Lansdowne MS. 639, fos. 25 (twice), 25^v, 28^v, 29^v, 30^v; H.E.H. Ellesmere MS. 2652, fo. 3^v.

46 Guy, *The Cardinal's Court*, 52–8.

47 B.L. Lansdowne MS. 639, fo. 58^v; H.E.H. Ellesmere MS. 2652, fo. 3^v.

48 B.L. Hargrave MS. 216, fo. 130; B.L. Lansdowne MS. 639, fo. 58; H.E.H. Ellesmere MS. 2652, fo. 3^v.

49 Guy, *The Cardinal's Court*, 72–8, 88–90.

50 STAC 2/9/186; STAC 10/4, Pt. 2, fos. 316–27; 10/4, Pt. 5, fo. 21 (twice); B.L. Lansdowne MS. 639, fos. 25–30.

51 B.L. Lansdowne MS. 639, fo. 53^v; H.E.H. Ellesmere MS. 2652, fo. 4.

52 STAC 10/4, Pt. 5, fo. 21; B.L. Lansdowne MS. 639, fo. 57.

53 Bodleian Library, Tanner MS. 101, fo. 62; B.L. Lansdowne MS. 639, fo. 5^v.

54 B.L. Lansdowne MS. 639, fo. 5^v.

55 STAC 10/4, Pt. 2, fo. 317^v. The entry dated 24 June 1525 reads: 'It is this daye ordred that in case John Anable doo not replye to Starkey to morrow, then he to be dismissed'.

56 B.L. Lansdowne MS. 639, fo. 5^v.

57 I have not found a *subpoena* to rejoin in the pre-1558 Star Chamber archive, but the writ may have been in use then.

58 B.L. Lansdowne MS. 639, fo. 6.

59 *Ibid.*

60 *Ibid.*

61 STAC 2/32/88.

62 Bayne and Dunham, *Select Cases in the Council of Henry VII*, civ–v. Material not available to Bayne at the time of his research confirms this account: STAC 10/4, Pts. 1–10; 10/8. See appendix D for Henry VII sub-numbers.

63 Witnesses examined by a clerk in Wolsey's chancellorship were first sworn before the chancellor. STAC 2/3/21, 23–5, 266–71, 32/loose

paper (unlisted fragments in box 2); H.E.H. Ellesmere MS. 2652, fo. 16^v. For examinations by councillors out of court, see STAC 2/8/49–50; 21/45; 31/loose paper (unlisted fragments in box 2).

64 STAC 2/18/16; 23/222; 29/loose paper (unlisted fragments in box 2); STAC 10/4, Pt. 2, fo. 321; H.E.H. Ellesmere MS. 2652, fo. 11.

65 STAC 4/11/48 (interrogatories to be administered to two witnesses who were to be examined after publication *ex parte* William Prewet).

66 The court's mature procedure is explained in B.L. Lansdowne MS. 639, fo. 8^v.

67 Guy, *The Cardinal's Court*, 93–105.

68 *Ardern* v. *Willoughby*, STAC 2/2/18–23, 24/411; *Legh* v. *Massy*, STAC 2/21/197; *Isot* v. *Carmynowe*, STAC 2/19/196; *Ap John Gruff* v. *Gryffith*, STAC 2/33/44; *Tredeneck* v. *Hamley*, STAC 2/18/76, 26/242; *Pigot* v. *Giggeney*, STAC 2/34/115; *Lewes* v. *Trentham*, STAC 2/21/199, 200, 235.

69 *Ardren* v. *Ardren*, STAC 2/2/1–8, 12–17, 22/275; *Bishop of St. Asaph* v. *Ap Gryffyth*, STAC 2/2/76–8; *Babington* v. *Rolleston*, STAC 2/3/19–20; *Crowche* v. *Mussell*, STAC 2/11/74–9, 13/137A, 25/34.

70 STAC 3/6/47.

71 Clerk of the process in Star Chamber.

72 B.L. Lansdowne MS. 639, fo. 7.

73 *Ibid.*, fo. 9; Bayne and Dunham, *Select Cases in the Council of Henry VII*, cvi–viii.

74 For instance, Lord Paget, who had antagonised the duke of Northumberland, was hauled into Star Chamber on 16 June 1552 for alleged corruption as chancellor of the duchy of Lancaster. Upon the reading by the attorney-general of the information against him, Paget confessed his offence. He had sold timber for his own profit, and taken fines on renewing and granting leases. Yet the true reason for his disgrace was to enable Northumberland to replace him with Sir John Gates. Thus Paget was compliant. After confessing, he submitted to the king's mercy on his knees, requesting the judges to be mediators for him in securing the remission of his sentence. He resigned his office, which was the main object of the exercise. He was bound in a recognisance of £1200 to pay a fine of £6000. However, within six months he had secured a pardon for all except crown debts, and was permitted to compound for his fine. In April 1553 part of the amount still due from him was remitted, and he was restored to favour. B.L. Harleian MS. 2143, fos. 6^v–7; *D.N.B.* See also examples cited by Guy, *The Cardinal's Court*, 72–8.

75 STAC 2/33/43 (bill of costs).

76 B.L. Harleian MS. 2143, fo. 5^v.

77 STAC 2/4/98–108.

78 STAC 2/16/192.

79 T. G. Barnes, 'Star Chamber and the Sophistication of the Criminal Law', *Criminal Law Review* (1977), 316–26.

80 H.E.H. Ellesmere MS. 2652, fos. 8^v, 14^v.

81 H.E.H. Ellesmere MS. 2655, fo. 12.

82 H.E.H. Ellesmere MS. 2652, fo. 14.

83 H.E.H. Ellesmere MS. 2768, fo. 25.

84 *Ibid.*

85 William Prynne, the lawyer and antiquary, was tried in 1634 for writing and publishing his 'Histriomastix: the Players Scourge'. See S. R. Gardiner (*ed.*), *Documents relating to the Proceedings against William Prynne* (London, Camden Society, 1877). A much fuller account of the Star Chamber proceedings in the case was given in

Sir John Clotworthy's MS. which described the sittings of the court from 24 January to 18 June 1634. This filled some 270 pages of manuscript. It was sold at Sotheby's sale of 21 March 1966, lot 200.

86 A. Fliche, C. Thouzellier, and Y. Azais, *La Chrétienté romaine, 1198–1274, Histoire de L'Eglise depuis les origines jusqu'à nos jours*, vol. 10 (Paris, 1950), 300–2.

87 B.L. Harleian MS. 2143, fos. 3^v–6; H.E.H. Ellesmere MS. 2768, fo. 25; Guy, *The Cardinal's Court*, 117.

88 B.L. Harleian MS. 2143, fo. 5. For Wolsey's punishments, see B.L. Lansdowne MS. 639, fos. 47^v, 49, 56; H.E.H. Ellesmere MSS. 479, 2652, fo. 14^v.

89 See above, p. 95 n. 74.

90 Guy, *The Cardinal's Court*, 116.

91 *Ibid*.

92 B.L. Harleian MS. 2143, fo. 1.

93 *Ibid*., fo. 1^v.

94 *Ibid*., fo. 1.

95 *Ibid*., fos. 1–11.

96 *Ibid*., fo. 4^v.

97 Guy, *The Cardinal's Court*, 52–8, 95.

98 Barnes, 'Star Chamber Litigants and their Counsel, 1596–1641', 11–13.

99 Guy, *The Cardinal's Court*, 95–105.

100 STAC 1/1/15; STAC 2/10/136, 136A; 14/45–6; 19/130; 20/9; 24/419; 27/81; B.L. Lansdowne MS. 639, fo. 24^v.

101 B.L. Harleian MS. 2143, fo. 2^v.

102 STAC 2/3/51; 5/72–6; 15/141–9; 29/150.

103 STAC 2/15/304–6; 18/305; 30/139.

104 STAC 2/13/150–4, 156–70.

105 STAC 2/20/328; 29/64.

106 STAC 10/4, Pt. 2 (certificate of Sir John Spelman and John Baldwin in *Heslop* v. *Menvyle*).

107 Guy, *The Cardinal's Court*, 105–8.

108 STAC 2/21/232; 23/252; 29/loose paper (unlisted fragment in box 2); STAC 10/18; *LP* ii. I. 1856; C 66/

634, m. 30 (exemplification for Elizabeth Flemmyng); *LP* iii. I. 278 (28).

109 STAC 2/12/65; 17/398, 407; 19/178, 373.

110 STAC 2/24/130.

111 STAC 2/5/51; 24/82.

112 STAC 2/12/85; 13/30–46, 135; 14/118–9; 24/82, 404; 33/43; B.L. Harleian MS. 2143, fos. 1–6. Guy, *The Cardinal's Court*, 114–15.

113 H.E.H. Ellesmere MS. 2652, fo. 5; B.L. Harleian MS. 2143, fos. 1–6, 69^v. Damages were not frequently awarded before 1529, but had become commoner by 1550. Guy, *The Cardinal's Court*, 115.

114 Guy, *The Cardinal's Court*, 108–9, 116–17, 128–30. B.L. Harleian MS. 2143, fos. 1^v, 6, 69–70; B.L. Lansdowne MS. 639, fo. 22; H.E.H. Ellesmere MS. 2757.

115 STAC 2/1/39; 5/51; 13/30–46; 17/399; 19/178; 30/126; B.L. Harleian MS. 2143, fos. 6^v–7.

116 B.L. Lansdowne MS. 639, fo. 22^v.

117 STAC 2/16/17–18; 19/304; SP 1/236, fos. 45–6; *LP Add*. 624 (2); B.L. Harleian MS. 2143, fo. 69^v.

118 Guy, *The Cardinal's Court*, 129.

119 B.L. Harleian MS. 2143, fo. 69^v; B.L. Lansdowne MS. 639, fos. 22^v, 55; H.E.H. Ellesmere MS. 2652, fo. 9^v; H.E.H. Ellesmere MS. 2655, fo. 13; H.E.H. Ellesmere MS. 2659.

120 Guy, *The Cardinal's Court*, 115, 129.

121 E 163/9/26; B.L. Lansdowne MS. 639, fo. 48; H.E.H. Ellesmere MS. 479; H.E.H. Ellesmere MS. 2652, fo. 1.

122 STAC 2/15/116; 31/142; B.L. Lansdowne MS. 639, fo. 26^v; H.E.H. Ellesmere MS. 2652, fo. 11; H.E.H. Ellesmere MS. 2655, fo. 13.

Chapter 4   Analysis of Star Chamber Proceedings

1   Guy, 'The Development of Equitable Jurisdictions, 1450–1550', 80–6.
2   For the best attempt at a case-unification method of description and analysis, see T. G. Barnes (ed.), *List and Index to the Proceedings in Star Chamber for the Reign of James I (1603–1625) in the Public Record Office, London, Class STAC 8*, 3 vols. (Chicago, 1975).
3   See above, pp. 29–35.
4   H.E.H. Ellesmere MS. 2655, fo. 10; Guy, *The Cardinal's Court*, 30–3, 119–31.
5   Guy, *The Cardinal's Court*, 31–5.
6   For this sample of 473 suits, see *ibid.*, 51–72. Nine official prosecutions are excluded from the present discussion. They are analysed *ibid.*, 72–8.
7   Cases of forcible entry, dispossession by violence, forcible detainder, assault, battery, false imprisonment, trespass to chattels etc. amount to thirteen per cent of the total sample of cases.
8   Guy, *The Cardinal's Court*, 61.
9   *Ibid.*, 65–6.
10   *Ibid.*, 67–71.
11   *Ibid.*, 53, 71–2.
12   H.E.H. Ellesmere MS. 2768, fos. 12–20^v; B.L. Hargrave MS. 216, fos. 178–80. The subjects listed were followed by folio references to an original book of precedents for the reigns of Henry VII and Henry VIII which is no longer extant. The surviving list was probably William Mill's index to this book of precedents. The original book of precedents was probably made up from the Council registers.
13   The table is compiled from the list in H.E.H. Ellesmere MS. 2768. In the original book of precedents, Warham's chancellorship extended to fo. 14, since 'The fraudulent taking away of goods' must refer to *Fraunces* v. *Sesson*, a leading case about carriers who broke bulk: STAC 2/15/296–300; 26/122, 417; 29/loose papers (bundle of fragments). Wolsey's chancellorship had begun by fo. 15, as 'The discretion of men by office found idiots' refers to William Dawvenande's case: a copy of the decree in this case is in E 208/19 (bundle). Since the subjects from 'Riots, misdemeanors, rescues, forcible entries' onwards to Dawvenande's case have duplicate references to fo. 16, or duplicate entries which were definitely within the limits of Wolsey's chancellorship, they may safely be included in the table. Wolsey's years were still under discussion on fo. 18, since 'The weringe of weapons in Westminster Hall & other courts forbidden by proclamations' refers to the proclamation of 18 October 1524: *Tudor Royal Proclamations*, ed. P. L. Hughes and J. F. Larkin (New Haven, 1964), i. 145. However, More's chancellorship had apparently begun part-way down fo. 19, as 'Admonition to the Londoners, Aldermen, for observing of laws' probably refers to the gathering in the Star Chamber on 1 February 1530. The precedents on fo. 20 were undoubtedly derived from the second Council register of Henry VIII, which covered the 1530s. In compiling the table, duplicate entries in the original list have been omitted.
14   H.E.H. Ellesmere MS. 2768, fo. 29^v.
15   B.L. Harleian MS. 2143, fo. 69.
16   *Ibid.*, fo. 1^v.
17   Skelton, 'The Court of Star Chamber in the Reign of Queen Elizabeth', Part 1, pp. 137–43; Barnes, 'Star Chamber and the Sophistication of the Criminal

Law', *Criminal Law Review* (1977), 316–26.

18 B.L. Harleian MS. 2143, fo. 1ᵛ.

19 STAC 2/5/51.

20 Guy, *The Cardinal's Court*, 96–7, 106–7, 127–31. For a cautious decree of Sir Thomas Audley pronounced on 10 July 1532, see STAC 2/17/407.

21 The charges against Wolsey are *LP* iv. III. 5749 (pp. 2550–3); 5750 (pp. 2555, 2557, 2562); 6075 (pp. 2712–14).

22 H.E.H. Ellesmere MS. 2768, fo. 29ᵛ.

23 *Ibid.*

24 H.E.H. Ellesmere MS. 2652, fos. 9ᵛ, 16ᵛ.

25 *Ibid.*, fo. 17.

26 This sample of cases was made by Skelton, 'The Court of Star Chamber in the Reign of Queen Elizabeth', Part 1, pp. 194–5, and full list of cases in Part 2. While the cases were identified by Skelton, the present analysis, however, is my own. I have followed the system of classification and description suggested by Barnes, 'Star Chamber Litigants and their Counsel, 1596–1641', 13. The value of Barnes's method is that, while faithfully reporting the shift from civil to criminal jurisdiction that characterised Star Chamber in Elizabeth's reign, it none the less retains comprehension of the essentially civil ends that motivated litigants who appeared in the court, notably their property ends. Barnes shows that even crimes against justice were linked to the litigants' proprietary concerns, 'because together with forgery and fraud they constituted the chief opportunity for mounting collateral actions touching other courts and impeaching other suits' (p. 13). It should be noted that the 1558–9 case sample made by Skelton is not exactly comparable to that made by

the present writer for Wolsey's chancellorship. I followed here and in my *Cardinal's Court* the case-unification method of analysis and description for Wolsey's years recommended by Barnes (see above n. 2). Miss Skelton located 72 cases for England and Wales filed in Elizabeth's first regnal year, but five cases were counted under two separate subject headings, owing to the difficulty of classifying them under a unified system. But it is not thought that this discrepancy, by which 72 cases are turned into 77 entries, seriously affects the discussion. Percentages are rounded up or down to the nearest whole number.

27 No extortion case was filed in 1558–9; Skelton, 'The Court of Star Chamber in the Reign of Queen Elizabeth', Part 1, pp. 194–5. For abduction, see Barnes, 'Star Chamber Litigants and their Counsel, 1596–1641', 13.

28 H.E.H. Ellesmere MS. 2768, fos. 28–9. Notes added by the side of these subjects in the hand of William Mill have been omitted. They mostly concern punishments inflicted by Star Chamber for the various offences. It is perhaps Mill's hand which added, too, the remarks about title and possession quoted above on pp. 55–6. These appear on fo. 29ᵛ.

29 7 Edward VI, c. 5.

30 Barnes, 'Star Chamber and the Sophistication of the Criminal Law', 316–26.

31 The cases were identified by Skelton, 'The Court of Star Chamber in the Reign of Queen Elizabeth', Part 1, pp. 196–7, and full list of cases in Part 2. Again the present analysis is my own, based upon Skelton's sample. As with the 1558–9 sample, the system of classification and description recommended by Barnes has been

adopted. Miss Skelton located and listed 732 cases for England and Wales filed in Elizabeth's last full regnal year, but 51 cases were counted under two subject headings, making 783 entries within the present sample. Thus there is a slight discrepancy, as before, if true comparison with the unified system of analysis made for Wolsey's years is to be attempted. But the degree of error does not seem significant, especially in view of the size of the 1601–2 sample. Basic patterns are clearly established.

32 See above, p. 54; Guy, *The Cardinal's Court*, 53, 71.

33 Barnes, 'Star Chamber Litigants and their Counsel, 1596–1641', 13.

34 Skelton, 'The Court of Star Chamber in the Reign of Queen Elizabeth', Part 1, pp. 142–3.

35 STAC 5/C. 25/4; C. 58/25; Skelton, 'The Court of Star Chamber in the Reign of Queen Elizabeth', Part 1, p. 143.

36 G. Salgado, *The Elizabethan Underworld* (London, 1977), 21–2, 29–30, 33, 130. The term 'cony-catching' probably goes back in the form 'cunny catching' to swindles involving prostitutes. Young heirs would be dragged out of bed by angry 'husbands' to whom they were immediately obliged by an admixture of force and embarrassment to lease or convey their assets.

37 These offences against the state and public policy amount to 0.3 per cent of the total sample of cases.

38 The defamation suits are discussed by Skelton, 'The Court of Star Chamber in the Reign of Queen Elizabeth', Part 1, pp. 127–36.

39 R. R. Reid, *The King's Council in the North* (London, 1921); P. Williams, *The Council in the Marches of Wales under Elizabeth I* (Cardiff, 1958).

40 The sample comprises 821 cases filed under Wolsey. Case titles and references are listed by Guy, 'The Court of Star Chamber during Wolsey's Ascendancy' (Cambridge Ph.D thesis, unpublished. 1973), appendix 3. This sample is different from the 473 fully-documented suits used above (p. 52 and n. 6).

41 The sample is that described in n. 31 above.

42 Cornwall, Devon, Somerset, Gloucestershire, Wiltshire, Dorset.

43 Cheshire, Salop, Warwickshire, Derbyshire, Staffordshire, Herefordshire, Worcestershire.

44 Norfolk, Suffolk, Huntingdon-shire, Essex, Cambridgeshire.

45 Lincolnshire, Nottinghamshire, Leicestershire, Rutland, Northamptonshire, Bedfordshire, Hertfordshire, Buckinghamshire, Oxfordshire.

46 Northumberland, Durham, Cumberland, Westmorland, Lancashire, Yorkshire.

47 Kent, Surrey, Sussex, Hampshire, Berkshire.

48 Welsh counties, including Marcher lordships shired in 1536, plus Flint, Monmouth, and Marches of Wales.

49 Percentage rounded to nearest half point.

50 1341 plaintiffs from the sample of 821 Wolsey cases (see above n. 40). However, the status of 588 plaintiffs is untraceable. The Jacobean data are taken from Barnes, 'Star Chamber Litigants and their Counsel, 1596–1641', 10.

51 STAC 2/18/15; 31/104.

52 The mature court allowed a few suitors *in forma pauperis*, but their bills were sometimes hit-and-run actions that abused the system. Barnes, 'Star Chamber Litigants and their Counsel, 1596–1641', 14.

53 STAC 2/12/85; Bayne and Dunham, *Select Cases in the Council of Henry VII*, 111.

54 H.E.H. Ellesmere MSS. 2678, 2680.

55 Compiled from STAC 2/8/231–3, 275; 13/30–46; 14/188–9; 15/96; 20/172; 24/404; 31/loose paper (bundle of unlisted fragments); 33/43; STAC 10/4, Pt. 2 (unlisted papers marked 'formerly REQ 3/18'); SP 1/233, fo. 274 (*LP Add.* 402).

56 Based on the list in H.E.H. Ellesmere MS. 2683 (dated 3 Dec. 1597). But I have added the estimated costs, not mentioned in the Ellesmere document, incurred for the purchase of process and injunctions. These are not mentioned because the Ellesmere paper concerns the clerk's fees, not those of the process officials. The costs of process are taken from B.L. Lansdowne MS. 639, fo. 21ᵛ. Since these are the amounts fixed by Egerton in 1598, they are, if anything, lower than the fees actually charged the previous year. We can only guess at the fees charged by the court's usher and other doorkeepers in 1597. I am unsure what fees were charged to the few plaintiffs allowed to sue *in forma pauperis*. However, they included a fee of 4d. per day to the clerk: 'the fee of *post diem* for every day' (H.E.H. Ellesmere MS. 2683).

BIBLIOGRAPHY

I Manuscripts

Public Record Office:

STAC 1 (2 bundles); STAC 2 (35 bundles); STAC 3 (8 bundles); STAC 4 (11 bundles); STAC 10 (21 bundles).

SP 1 (vols. 1–60, 231–246); SP 2 (vol. A).

REQ 1/1–5; REQ 3 (38 bundles).

C 66/627–628; C 82/474; C 244/138–182; C 253/53–56.

E 28/93; E 28/96; E 36/124; E 36/125; E 36/194; E 36/215; E 36/216; E 101/414/16; E 101/517/11; E 137/143/2; E 163/9/20; E 163/24/9; E 208/19; E 315/313A; E 407/51–55.

PC 2/1–2

British Library:

Additional MSS. 4520; 4521; 5485; 11,681; 21,480; 21,481; 24,926; 26,647; 28,201; 36,111; 36,112; 41,661.

Cotton MSS. Titus B. i; Titus B. iv; Titus B. v; Vespasian C. xiv; Vespasian F. ix; Vespasian F. xiii.

Hargrave MSS. 216; 237; 250; 251; 290; 482.

Harleian MSS. 297; 305; 425; 444; 736; 829; 859; 1200; 1226; 1576; 1689; 2143; 3504; 4272; 4274; 5350; 6235; 6256; 6448; 6811; 6815; 7161.

Lansdowne MSS. 1; 69; 83; 160; 232; 254; 622; 639; 830; 905.

Stowe MSS. 145; 418; 419.

Henry E. Huntington Library:
Ellesmere MSS. 436; 438; 439; 440; 446; 465; 479; 481; 485; 486; 495; 1169; 2562; 2652; 2653; 2654; 2655; 2656; 2657; 2658; 2659; 2661; 2670; 2683; 2685; 2725; 2739; 2740; 2746; 2757; 2759; 2761; 2764; 2765; 2766; 2767; 2768; 2769; 2810; 7921.

Guildhall, London:
MS. 1751.

All Souls College, Oxford:
MSS. 178a; 178b; 256; 258.

Bodleian Library:
MS. Carte 119; Douce 66; Eng. hist. c. 304; Tanner 101.

Corpus Christi College, Oxford:
MS. 196.

St. Edmund Hall, Oxford:
MS. 3.

Cambridge University Library:
MSS. Additional 3105; Dd. 11. 58; Dd. 11. 81; Gg. 5. 18; Ii. 6. 54; Kk. 6. 22; Ll. 3. 3; Ll. 4. 10; Mm. 5. 12.

Folger Shakespeare Library:
MSS. 511121.1 (V. a. 207); V. b. 179; V. b. 205.

II Printed Material
Adair, E. R. (*ed.*), *The Sources for the History of the Council in the Sixteenth and Seventeenth Centuries.* London 1924.

Baker, J. H. (*ed.*), *The Reports of Sir John Spelman.* 2 vols, London, Selden Society, 1977–78.

Baldwin, J. F., *The King's Council in England during the Middle Ages.* Oxford 1913.

Barnes, T. G., 'The Archives and Archival Problems of the Elizabethan and Early Stuart Star Chamber', *Journal of the Society of Archivists*, ii (1963), 345–60.

–, 'Due Process and Slow Process in the Late Elizabethan-Early Stuart Star Chamber', *American Journal of Legal History*, vi (1962), 221–49, 315–46.

–, 'Star Chamber Mythology', *American Journal of Legal History*, v (1961), 1–11.

–, Review in *Speculum*, xxiv (1959), 650–51.

–, 'Star Chamber Litigants and their Counsel, 1596–1641', in *Legal Records and the Historian*, ed. J. H. Baker. London 1978, 7–28.

–, 'Mr. Hudson's Star Chamber', in *Tudor Rule and Revolution*, ed. DeLloyd J. Guth and J. W. McKenna. Cambridge 1982, 285–308.

–, 'Star Chamber and the Sophistication of the Criminal Law', *Criminal Law Review* (1977), 316–26.

–, 'A Cheshire Seductress, Precedent, and a "Sore Blow" to Star Chamber', in *On the Laws and Customs of England*, ed. M. S. Arnold, T. A. Green, S. A. Scully and S. D. White. Chapel Hill 1981, 359–382.

–, (*ed.*), *List and Index to the Proceedings in Star Chamber for the Reign of James I (1603–1625) in the Public Record Office, London, Class STAC 8.* 3 vols., Chicago 1975.

Bayne, C. G. and Dunham, W. H. (*eds.*), *Select Cases in the Council of Henry VII.* London, Selden Society, 1958.

Bell, H. E., *An Introduction to the History and Records of the Court of Wards and Liveries.* Cambridge 1953.

Brayley, E. W. and Britton, J., *History of the Ancient Palace and the Late House of Parliament at Westminster.* London 1836.

Briquet, C. M., *Les Filigranes,* ed. A. Stevenson. Amsterdam, Paper Publications Society, 1968.

Brown, A. L., *The Early History of the Clerkship of the Council.* Glasgow, Glasgow University Publications NS 131, 1969.

Burn, J. S., *The Star Chamber.* London 1870.

Campbell, Lord, *Lives of the Lord Chancellors and Keepers of the Great Seal of England.* London, 5th ed., 1868.

Carlton, W. N. C., *Notes on the Bridgewater House Library.* New York 1918.

Cavendish, G., *The Life and Death of Cardinal Wolsey,* ed. R. S. Sylvester. London, Early English Text Society, 1959.

Chrimes, S. B., *Henry VII.* London 1972.

Collier, J. P. (*ed.*), *The Egerton Papers.* London, Camden Society, 1840.

Cokayne, G. E., *The Complete Peerage of England Scotland Ireland Great Britain and the United Kingdom,* rev. ed. by V. Gibbs *et al.* London 1910–.

Crompton, R., *L'Authoritie et Jurisdiction des Courts de la Majestie de la Roygne.* London 1594.

Dunham, W. H., 'The Ellesmere Extracts from the "Acta Consilii" of King Henry VIII', *English Historical Review*, lviii (1943), 301–18.

–, 'Henry VIII's Whole Council and its Parts', *Huntington Library Quarterly*, vii (1943), 7–46.

–, 'The Members of Henry VIII's Whole Council, 1509–27', *English Historical Review*, lix (1944), 187–210.

–, 'Wolsey's Rule of the King's Whole Council', *American Historical Review*, xlix (1944), 644–62.

Ellis, H. (*ed.*), *Original Letters, Illustrative of English History.* London 1824–46.

Elton, G. R., *Studies in Tudor and Stuart Politics and Government.* 3 vols., Cambridge 1974, 1983.

–, *Policy and Police.* Cambridge 1972.

–, *Star Chamber Stories.* London 1958.

–, *The Tudor Constitution.* Cambridge, 2nd ed. 1982.

–, *The Tudor Revolution in Government*. Cambridge 1953.

Foss, E., *Judges of England with Sketches of their Lives and Notices connected with the Courts at Westminster*. London 1848–64.

Gordon, M. D., 'The Invention of a Common Law Crime: Perjury and the Elizabethan Courts', *American Journal of Legal History*, xxiv (1980), 145–170.

–, 'The Perjury Statute of 1563: a case history of confusion', *Proceedings of the American Philosophical Society*, cxxiv (1980), 438–454.

Guy, J. A., *The Cardinal's Court*. Hassocks 1977.

–, *The Public Career of Sir Thomas More*. Brighton 1980.

–, 'Wolsey's Star Chamber: a Study in Archival Reconstruction', *Journal of the Society of Archivists*, v (1975), 169–80.

–, 'The Privy Council: Revolution or Evolution?', in *Revolution Reassessed*, ed. D. R. Starkey and C. Coleman. Oxford forthcoming.

–, 'The Development of Equitable Jurisdictions, 1450–1550', in *Law, Litigants and the Legal Profession*, ed. E. W. Ives and A. H. Manchester. London 1983, 80–86.

Hake, E., *Epiekeia, a Dialogue on Equity in Three Parts*, ed. D. E. C. Yale. New Haven 1953.

Hall, E., *The Triumphant Reigne of Kyng Henry the VIII*, ed. C. Whibley. London 1904.

Harding, A., *The Law Courts of Medieval England*. London 1973.

Hasler, P. W. (*ed.*), *The House of Commons, 1558–1603*. 3 vols., London 1981.

Hawarde, J., *Les Reportes del Cases in Camera Stellata, 1593–1609*, ed. W. P. Baildon. London 1894.

Hearne, T. (*ed.*), *A Collection of Curious Discourses Written by Eminent Antiquaries upon Several Heads in our English Antiquities*. London 1771.

Hill, L. M. (*ed.*), *The Ancient State, Authoritie, and Proceedings of the Court of Requests by Sir Julius Caesar*. Cambridge 1975.

Hoak, D. E., *The King's Council in the Reign of Edward VI*. Cambridge 1976.

Holdsworth, W. S., *A History of English Law*, vol. i (7th ed. by S. B. Chrimes, London 1956); vols. iv and v (3rd ed. 1945).

Hudson, W., 'A Treatise of the Court of Star Chamber'. In F. Hargrave (*ed.*), *Collectanea Juridica*, ii, 1–239. London 1791–2.

Hughes, P. L. and J. F. Larkin (*eds.*), *Tudor Royal Proclamations*, i, *The Early Tudors (1485–1553)*. New Haven 1964.

Jacob, G., *The Law Dictionary*, rev. ed. by T. E. Tomlins. London 1797.

Jones, W. J., *The Elizabethan Court of Chancery*. Oxford 1967.

Journals of the House of Lords. London 1846–.

Kerridge, E., *Agrarian Problems in the Sixteenth Century and After*. London 1969.

Lambarde, W., *Archeion: or, a Discourse upon the High Courts of Justice in England*, ed. C. H. McIlwain and P. L. Ward. Cambridge (Mass.) 1957.

Leadam, I. S. (*ed.*), *Select Cases before the King's Council in the Star Chamber commonly called the Court of Star Chamber A.D. 1477–1509*. London, Selden Society, 1903.

–, *Select Cases before the King's Council in the Star Chamber commonly called the Court of Star Chamber A.D. 1509–1544*. London, Selden Society, 1911.

–, *Select Cases in the Court of Requests A.D. 1497–1569*. London, Selden Society, 1898.

Lehmberg, S. E., *Sir Thomas Elyot*. Austin 1964.

–, 'Star Chamber: 1485–1509', *Huntington Library Quarterly*, xxiv (1961), 189–214.

–, 'Sir Thomas Audley: a Soul as Black as Marble', in *Tudor Men and Institutions*, ed. A. J. Slavin. Baton Rouge 1972, 3–31.

Letters and Papers, Foreign and Domestic,

of the Reign of Henry VIII, ed. J. S. Brewer, J. Gairdner, R. H. Brodie. London 1862–1932.

Lodge, E. (ed.), Illustrations of British History . . . in the Reigns of Henry VIII, Edward VI, Mary, Elizabeth, and James I. London 1838.

Megarry, R. E., A Manual of the Law of Real Property, 2nd ed. London 1955.

Milsom, S. F. C., Historical Foundations of the Common Law. London 1969.

Nicolas, N. H. (ed.), Proceedings and Ordinances of the Privy Council of England, 1368–1542. 7 vols., London 1834–37.

Norburie, G., 'The Abuses and Remedies of Chancerie'. In F. Hargrave (ed.), A Collection of Tracts Relative to the Law of England, 425–448. London 1787.

Plucknett, T. F. T. and Barton, J. L. (eds.), St. German's Doctor and Student. London, Selden Society, 1974.

Pollard, A. F., 'Council, Star Chamber, and Privy Council under the Tudors', English Historical Review, xxxvii (1922), 337–60, 516–39; xxxviii (1923) 42–60.

–, 'The Growth of the Court of Requests', English Historical Review, lvi (1941), 300–3.

–, Wolsey. London 1929.

–, 'Wolsey and the Great Seal', Bulletin of the Institute of Historical Research, vii (1929), 85–97.

– and C. H. Williams, 'Council Memoranda in 1528', Bulletin of the Institute of Historical Research, v (1927), 23–27.

Powell, E., 'Arbitration and the Law in England in the Late Middle Ages', Transactions of the Royal Historical Society, 5th series xxxiii (1983), 49–67.

Public Record Office, List of Proceedings in the Court of Star Chamber, i, 1485–1558. Lists and Indexes, Original Series, No. 13. New York, Kraus Reprint Corporation, 1963.

– Proceedings in the Court of Star Chamber, i, 1485–1558. Lists and Indexes, Supplementary Series, No. 4.

New York, Kraus Reprint Corporation, 1966.

Register of Admissions to the Honourable Society of Middle Temple, i. London 1949.

Reid, R. R., The King's Council in the North. London 1921.

'A Replication of a Serjeant at the Laws of England, to certain Points alledged by a Student of the said Laws of England, in a Dialogue in English between a Doctor of Divinity and the Said Student'. In Doctor and Student, ed. W. Muchall. London 1815.

Reports and Calendars issued by the Royal Commission on Historical Manuscripts. London 1870–.

Reports of the Deputy Keeper of the Public Records. London 1840–88.

Richardson, W. C., Tudor Chamber Administration, 1485–1547. Baton Rouge 1952.

Sanders, G. W., Orders of the High Court of Chancery. London 1845.

Schanz, G., Englische Handelspolitik gegen Ende des Mittelalters. Leipzig 1881.

Schofield, R. S., 'The Geographical Distribution of Wealth in England 1334–1649', Economic History Review, 2nd series, xviii (1965), 483–510.

Scofield, C. L., A Study of the Court of Star Chamber. Chicago 1900.

–, 'Accounts of Star Chamber Dinners, 1593–4', American Historical Review, v (1899), 85–95.

Seyssel, Claude de, The Monarchy of France, trans. J. H. Hexter and ed. D. R. Kelley. New Haven 1981.

Simpson, A. W. B., An Introduction to the History of the Land Law. Oxford 1961.

Skeel, C. A. J., The Council in the Marches of Wales. London 1904.

–, 'The Council of the West', Transactions of the Royal Historical Society, 4th Series, iv (1921), 62–80.

Smith, T., De Republica Anglorum. London, Scolar Press, 1970.

Somerville, R., 'Henry VII's "Council Learned in the Law" ', English Historical Review, liv (1939), 427–42.

The Statutes of the Realm, ed. A. Luders *et al.* London, Record Commission, 1810–28.

Webb, E. A., *The Records of St. Bartholomew's Priory and the Church and Parish of St. Bartholomew the Great West Smithfield.* Oxford 1921.

Williams, C. H., 'The so-called Star Chamber Act', *History*, new series, xv (1930), 129–35.

Williams, P., *The Council in the Marches of Wales under Elizabeth I*. Cardiff 1958.

–, 'The Star Chamber and the Council in the Marches of Wales, 1558–1603', *Bulletin of the Board of Celtic Studies*, xvi (1956), 287–97.

–, *The Tudor Regime*. Oxford 1979.

Wolffe, B. P., *The Crown Lands 1461 to 1536*. London 1970.

Yale, D. E. C. (*ed.*), Lord Nottingham's 'Manual of Chancery Practice' and 'Prolegomena of Chancery and Equity'. Cambridge 1965.

Youings, J. A., 'The Council of the West', *Transactions of the Royal Historical Society*, 5th series, x (1960), 41–60.

III Dissertations

Knox, D. A., 'The Court of Requests in the Reign of Edward VI'. Cambridge, Ph.D. thesis, 1974.

Lemasters, G. A., 'The Privy Council in the Reign of Queen Mary I'. Cambridge, Ph.D. thesis, 1971.

Skelton, E., 'The Court of Star Chamber in the Reign of Queen Elizabeth'. London, M.A. thesis, 1931.

INDEX

Abduction, 47, 58, 60

Abuse of legal procedure, 53; *see also* Embracery; Juries, corrupt verdicts of; Perjury; Subornation

Actions *see individual subjects*

Adene, Thomas, 25–6

Affidavits, 12–14, 20, 22, 32, 34, 39–41, 50, 63–5

Allen, Dr. John, 31

Answers, 12–13, 15–16, 21, 24, 26–8, 39–42, 45, 48, 63–4

Appearances, 12–14, 20–1, 23, 34, 38–9, 41, 43, 45, 49, 63

Arbitration, 2, 10, 40, 47–9

Assault, 26, 52–3, 57, 59

Assistant clerk of the Council, 11–12; *see also* Eden, Richard; Elyot, Sir Thomas; Lee, Richard

Attachment, writ of, 14, 38, 41, 63–4

Attorney, 14–16, 45, 62, 64; admissions to, 12–13, 20–1, 34, 41, 63–4; *see also* Beere, John; Besson, Anthony; Goad, John; Grimstone, Edward; Hexte, William; Jones, Walter; Mill, William, junior; Mill, William, senior; Mills, Thomas; Taverner, John; Valentine, John; Wrightington, Edward

Attorney-general, 21, 37, 41, 45, 47

Audley, Sir Thomas (lord chancellor 1533–44), 9, 44, 48, 98 n20

Bacon, Sir Francis (lord chancellor 1618–21), 65

Bacon, Sir Nicholas (lord keeper 1558–79), 8–9

Baldeswell, John (clerk of the Council 1485–92), 11

Banishment, 33

Barretry, 55

Battery, 53, 58, 97 n7

Beere, John (attorney *c*. 1600), 16

Bellowe, Patrick, 31, 93 n30

Besson, Anthony (attorney *c*. 1600), 16

Bigamy, 26

Bill of complaint, 10, 12–15, 21–8, 37–42, 45, 48, 53, 57, 63

Blasphemy, 46

Blundell, George, 57

—, Nicholas, 56

Blundell v. *Molyneux*, 56

Breach of contract, 54

Brecknocke, William, 40

Brereton, Sir William, 47

Bribery, 29, 59

British Library, 29–35, 56, 78–9

Brown, Richard (steward of Star Chamber 1536–53), 17

Browne, George, 44

—, Sir Humphrey, 33

Butler, Richard, 40

Calverley, Sir Walter, 47

Certiorari, writ of, 13, 64

Chaloner, Robert, 44

Champerty, 53, 58

Chancellor *see* Lord chancellor

Chancery, court of, 4, 6, 11, 14, 22, 24–7, 29, 38–9, 47, 50, 57, 65, 73, 77, 86 n5, 91 n9, 93 n27

Chapter House, Westminster, 19, 23–4

Charles I (king of England), 19–20

Cheyney, Sir Thomas, 9

Cholmeley v. *Holford*, 57

Clayburgh, William, 11

Clerk of the Council, 7–8, 11–14, 20–5, 29, 38–41, 43, 49, 64–5, 92 n11, 94 n35, 100 n56; *see also* Baldeswell, John; Eden, Richard; Eden, Thomas, Marshe, Thomas; Meautis, John; Mill, William, junior; Rydon, Robert

Clerk of the files, 13–14

Clerk of the process, 14–15; *see also* Cotton, Bartholomew; Cotton, Thomas uncle of Bartholomew; Cotton, Thomas son of Bartholomew; Pope, Sir Thomas; Smyth, William

Commission of rebellion, 38, 63–4
Commissions, 10, 12, 14–15, 19, 23–5,
  32–4, 40, 43–5, 48–9, 62–4
Common law, 25–7, 38–9, 44, 49, 53,
  55–7
Common Pleas, chief justices of, 7–8
Complaint, bill of *see* Bill of complaint
Confessions, 37, 45
Congresse, Rafe, 25
Conseil du Roi, 7
Contempt, 12, 34, 38, 41, 47, 50, 53–4,
  58, 64, 93 n23
Conversion, 53
Conyngesby, Sir Humfrey, 46
Copinger, John, 47
Corrupt juries *see* Juries, corrupt verdicts
  of
Corruption of officials, 53, 58
Costs, 12, 14, 21, 27, 33, 38–9, 42, 45,
  47, 50, 62–5
Cotton, Bartholomew (clerk of the
  process), 15
—, Isaac, 14
—, Thomas uncle of Bartholomew (clerk
  of the process), 15
—, Thomas son of Bartholomew (clerk of
  the process), 15
Council *see* King's Council
Council attendant *see* King's Council
Counsel, 28, 45, 62, 88 n46, 90 n79
Cozenage, 58, 60
Criminal cases, 1, 22, 28, 35, 38, 40–1,
  45, 47, 51, 53–4, 58–60, 79, 91 n6,
  98 n26
Cromwell, Thomas, 1st lord Cromwell,
  earl of Essex, 6–7
Cucking-stool, 46
Curwen, Agnes, 46

Damages, 33, 47, 50, 65
Damsell, Sir John, 62
Darcy, Sir Arthur, 44
Darcy v. *Tempest et al.*, 44
Debt, 54
Decrees *see* Orders and decrees
Dedimus potestatem, writ of, 12, 19, 21,
  22, 24–5, 34, 40–1, 43–4, 48, 63–5
Defamation, 54, 59–60
Demurrer, 14, 39
Denman, Francis, 15
Deodands, 37

Depositions, 12, 14, 21, 23–5, 28–9, 43,
  45, 48
Derby, Thomas (clerk of the Privy
  Council), 12
Detinue, 53
Dispossession, 53, 97 n7
Doddington, John (steward of Star
  Chamber 1572–85), 17
Dudley, John, earl of Warwick, duke of
  Northumberland, 8–10, 95 n74

Easements dispute, 54
Ecclesiastical courts, 28, 46
Eden, Richard (assistant clerk of the
  Council *c.* 1509–12; clerk 1512–30),
  11–13, 23, 31, 83 n68, 84 n77, 88 n30,
  90 n78
—, Thomas nephew of Richard (clerk of
  the Council 1530–67), 11–12, 23,
  88 n31, 93 n30
Edward III (king of England), 1–2, 16
Edward IV (king of England), 2, 20
Edward VI (king of England), 8, 10, 38,
  44, 56–7
Egerton, Sir Thomas, lord Ellesmere
  (lord keeper 1596–1603; lord
  chancellor 1603–17), 9, 14–15, 29–32,
  34, 37–8, 57, 62–3
Elizabeth I (queen of England), 1, 8–9,
  13–14, 16, 21, 27–8, 34, 40, 42, 45, 47,
  54–62, 65
Ellesmere, lord *see* Egerton, Thomas
Ely, bishop of *see* Goodrich, Thomas
Elyot, Sir Thomas (assistant clerk of the
  Council *c.* 1526–30), 11, 13, 23,
  83 n68, 84 n75, 87 n29
Embezzlement, 54, 59
Embracery, 52–3, 55, 58
Enclosure, 44, 54
Engrossing, 46, 53
Essex, earl of *see* Cromwell, Thomas
Examinations, 12–16, 21, 23, 28–9,
  39–45, 48, 62–4, 91 n6
Exceptions, 27
Exchequer, 1, 22, 27, 34–5, 38; chief
  baron of, 8, 45
Execution, writ of, 50
Exile *see* Banishment
Extortion, 46, 54–5, 58–60

False accusation, 55
False imprisonment, 53, 97 n7
Felony, 53; *see also* Criminal cases
Fines, 1, 22, 32–4, 46–7, 58, 95 n74
Fitzjames, James, C.J.K.B., 46
Fleet prison, 27, 38–9, 41, 46–7, 50, 55, 57; warden of, 16
Forcible detainder, 53, 97 n7
Forcible entry, 26, 52–4, 58–9, 93 n29
Forestalling, 53
Forgery, 54, 58, 60
Fraud, 54, 58, 60
Frivolous suits, 9, 27, 32, 38–9

Gardiner, Stephen, bishop of Winchester (lord chancellor 1553–5), 10
Geographical distribution of suits, 60–1
Goad, John (attorney *c.* 1556), 16
Goodrich, Thomas, bishop of Ely (lord keeper 1551; lord chancellor 1552–3), 10
Gray's Inn, 13, 19, 21
Grimstone, Edward (attorney *c.* 1572), 16
Guilpin, Francis (steward of Star Chamber 1585–89), 17
Guisborough, Yorks, manor, 44

Harvey, Richard, 60
—, Thomas, 13
Hatton, Sir Christopher (lord chancellor 1587–91), 13
Hearing of suits, 45, 49, 65
Heath, Nicholas, archbishop of York (lord chancellor 1556–8), 9–10, 23
Henry IV (king of England), 2
Henry VI (king of England), 2, 20
Henry VII (king of England), 2–5, 12, 16, 27, 38, 40–1, 43, 56, 62
Henry VIII (king of England), 2–6, 8, 10, 12, 14, 25, 27–8, 30, 33–5, 38–42, 46, 49, 51, 54, 56, 58, 60, 62
Heresy, 10, 47
Hertford, earl of *see* Seymour, Edward
Hexte, William (attorney *c.* 1587), 16
Heydon, Henry, 26
Hillorye, Sebastian (steward of Star Chamber 1522–36), 17
Hudson, William, vii, 33–4, 78
Hunting offence, 54, 59
Huntington Library, 29–33, 51, 78

Illegal distress, 53
Imprisonment *see* Punishment
Information, 21, 37, 39, 95 n74
Injunctions, 12–13, 20, 32–4, 47, 50, 63–4
Interrogatories, 14, 21, 24, 27–9, 39–44
Interruption of family relations, 54
Ipswich, Suff, 46

James I (king of England), 9, 14, 47, 61–2, 65
Jones, Walter (attorney *c.* 1592), 16
Juries, corrupt verdicts of, 33, 47, 53, 55, 58, 60

King's almoner, 37
King's Bench, chief justices of, 7–8; secondary justice of, 46; *see also* Fitzjames, James
King's Council:
    acta, 12, 21, 31–2, 34, 54
    council attendant, 2–4, 6, 12
    councillors 'at large', 7–8
    medieval history, 1–2, 91 n2
    'ordinary' councillors, 10
    under Henry VII, 2, 4–5, 12
    under Henry VIII, 2–10, 12, 14
    under Edward VI, 8–11
    under Mary, 8–9
    under Elizabeth I, 2, 9
Kyneston, Edward, 40

Lambert, Henry, 49–50
Landlord and tenant disputes, 54, 56, 59
Law terms, 4, 6, 38, 40–1, 44, 48, 92 n18
Lee, Richard (assistant clerk of the Council 1516–*c.* 30), 11–13, 23, 83 n75, 87 n29
Libel, 58
Libri Intrationum, 30–4, 51, 54–5, 57–8
Lightfoot, John, 33–4
Lincoln, bishop of *see* Williams, John
London, 40, 43, 45–6, 48, 60–1; grocers of, 32; jury in, 47; recorder of, 46
Long Parliament, 2, 6, 65
Lord chancellor, role of, 8–10, 12, 21–2, 25, 30, 38, 41, 45, 47–9, 92 n11, 94 n63; *see also individual lord chancellors*

Maintenance, 47, 52–3, 55, 58, 60
Marshe, Thomas (clerk of the Council
    1567–87), 11, 88 n38
Mary I (queen of England), 8–10, 27, 34,
    39–40, 47, 56
Master of the rolls, 8
Mayhem, 55
Meautis, John (clerk of the Council
    1509–12), 11
Menyell, Robert, 44
Mercantile cases, 50
Messenger of Star Chamber, 16
Mill, William, junior (attorney c. 1555;
    clerk of the Council 1587–1608), 8, 11,
    13–14, 16, 22, 30, 33, 88 n35, 97 n12,
    98 n28
—, William, senior (attorney c. 1520), 16
Mills, Thomas (attorney c. 1592), 16,
    84 n91
Misdemeanour, 54, 58–9, 93 n27, n29;
    see also individual subjects
More, Sir Thomas (lord chancellor 1529–
    32), 6, 9, 12, 37, 46, 91 n9, 97 n13
Morgan, William, 25–6
Municipal and trade disputes, 53
Mynatt, Thomas, 13

Nores, Richard (usher of Star Chamber),
    15
Northumberland, duke of see Dudley,
    John
Norwich, Norf, 46
Norwiche, Robert, 32
Nuisance, 54

Oaths, 13, 27–8, 39, 44, 64–5
Officers' malfeasance, 37, 53, 58, 60
Onslow's Case, 2
Orders and decrees, 10, 12–15, 19–24,
    29, 32–4, 41, 47, 49–51, 54, 56–7,
    62–4, 79 n1

Paget, William, 7, 47, 95 n74
Palmer, Thomas (usher of Star
    Chamber), 15
Paulet, William, lord St. John (lord
    keeper 1547), 10
Payne, John, 49–50
Payne v. Lambert, 49
Perjury, 27, 29, 39, 47, 53–4, 58, 60
Pilgrimage of Grace, 7

Plommer, Sir Christopher, 31
Pope, Sir Thomas (clerk of the process),
    14–15
Posse comitatus, 50
Precedents, 12, 13, 23, 30, 32, 34, 44,
    89 n66, 97 n12, n13
Privy Council see King's Council
Privy seal, writ of, 21, 34, 38, 43, 63
Process in Star Chamber, 12–13, 20,
    23–5, 32, 37–8, 42, 59, 63; see also
    individual instruments
Procuration, 54–5, 58–60
Prynne's Case, 46
Publication, 43, 45, 49, 65
Pulton, Ferdinand, 2
Punishment, 29, 32–3, 38–9, 46–7, 50,
    57, 80 n13, 98 n28; see also
    Banishment; Cucking-stool; Fines;
    Fleet prison

Quibusdam certis de causis, writ of, 38

Real property suits, 26, 41, 47, 50, 52, 57
Receivership, 50
Recognisances, 12–13, 20–2, 34, 38, 41,
    47, 50, 63–4, 95 n74
Registrar of Star Chamber, 13–14
Regrating, 53
Rejoinder, 14, 21, 24, 27–8, 42, 89 n60
Replication, 14, 21, 24, 27–8, 42, 44, 48,
    89 n60
Requests, court of, 3–4, 6, 10–11, 24–5,
    62, 67, 71–2, 76–7, 86 n5; masters of,
    10; see also White Hall court
Rescue, 54
Resistance, 59
Rich, Richard, 1st lord Rich (lord
    chancellor 1547–51), 10
Richard II (king of England), 2
Riot and public order offences, 26, 41,
    47, 52–60, 92 n15, 93 n29; see also
    Forcible entry
Rules in Star Chamber, 13–15, 22, 64
Ryder family, 25
Rydon, Robert (clerk of the Council
    1492–1509), 11, 23, 87 n29
Ryseley, Robert, 57

St. Bartholomew's Close, London, 19, 35
St. John, lord see Paulet, William
Serjeant of the mace, 16

Sequestration, 50
Seymour, Edward, earl of Hertford,
   duke of Somerset (lord protector), 8
Smith, Sir Thomas, 8
Smyth, William (clerk of the process),
   14–15, 44
Smythe, Nicholas (steward of Star
   Chamber c. 1590), 17
Social status of litigants, 61–2
Somerset, duke of see Seymour, Edward
Southampton, earl of see Wriothesley, Sir
   Thomas
Southworth, Sir John, 47
Star Chamber:
   abolition of, 2, 6–7, 14, 19, 65
   buildings and furniture, 1–2
   business, 5, 9–10, 13, 28, 31, 41, 43,
      47, 51–60
   dinners, 16–17, 22
   judges, 2, 5, 7–9, 31, 34, 45, 56–7,
      91 n6
   office in Gray's Inn, 13, 15, 19, 21, 34
   officers, 11–17; see also individual
      officers of the court
   origins of the court, 2–3
   proceedings, 19–25, 51–65,
      appendices A–D
   procedure, 37–50
      records to 1558, 19–35; see also
      separate instruments
   registers of orders and decrees, 7, 9,
      12–13, 21–3, 29–34, 39, 49, 51, 54
   structure, 1–17
Statutes:
   3 Henry VII, c. 1, 2
   7 Edward VI, c. 5, 59
Staunton, William (steward of Star
   Chamber 1553–72), 17
Steward, 16–17; see also Brown, Richard;
   Doddington, John; Guilpin, Francis;
   Hillorye, Sebastian; Smythe,
   Nicholas; Staunton, William
Subornation, 29, 53, 55, 58, 60, 93 n27
Subpoena, writ of, 12, 14, 20–2, 24–5,
   34, 38, 63, 91 n9, 94 n35, n57
Subpoena ad audiendum iudicium, writ of,
   45, 63
Subpoena ad reiungendum, writ of, 42
Subpoena ad testificandum, writ of, 43, 63
Surrejoinder, 42

Taverner, John (attorney c. 1535), 16
Tempest, Sir John, 44
Testamentary disputes, 54
Throckmorton, Sir Nicholas, 47
—, Thomas, 57
Tithes disputes, 54, 56
Title cases, 21, 26, 28, 41, 47, 49–50,
   52–3, 55–8, 60, 79, 92 n17
Torts, 54
Tower of London, 31, 47, 50, 59; records
   in, 30
Trade disputes see Municipal and trade
   disputes
Treason, 47
Trentham, Thomas, 47
Trespass, 52; to chattels, 53, 97 n7

Under-clerkships, 13–15
Under-registrar, 14
Unlawful assembly see Riot and public
   order offences
Usher, 15, 100 n56; see also Nores,
   Richard; Palmer, Thomas

Valentine, John (attorney c. 1528), 16
Vavasour, Sir William, 44
Vesacreley, John, 46
Vowles's Case, 46

Walton, John, 25
Ward v. Ousley, 56
Wards and Liveries, court of, 24
Warwick, earl of see Dudley, John
Westminster, palace of, 1–2, 4, 12, 16,
   22, 26, 44–5, 49, 56; hall, 39, 97 n13
White Hall court (origins of court of
   Requests), 3, 6, 57
Whittingestall, Richard, 46
Williams, John, bishop of Lincoln (lord
   keeper 1621–25), 9, 60, 79 n1
Winchester, bishop of see Gardiner,
   Stephen
Witnesses, 12–13, 21, 24, 28–9, 39–40,
   42–5, 48, 63–4
Wolsey, Thomas, archbishop of York,
   legate a latere (lord chancellor 1515–
   29), 1, 4–7, 9, 11–12, 15–16, 27, 30–2,
   34, 38, 41, 47, 51–4, 56–62, 65, 71
Wrightington, Edward (attorney
   c. 1592), 16

Wriothesley, Sir Thomas, 1st lord
   Wriothesley, earl of Southampton
   (lord chancellor 1544–7), 10
Writs *see separate entries*
Wrongful arrest, 57, 59

Wyatt's rebellion, 47

York, archbishops of *see individual
   incumbents*

Printed in the UK for HMSO
Dd 737369   c.10   2/85   E&S 37796